BEFORE YOU BUY YOUR HOUSE OR APARTMENT—

HAVE YOU ASKED ALL THE RIGHT QUESTIONS?

Did you know that...

- blistered or bubbled paint can be a sign of rotting wood underneath?
- sagging or unlevel steps might indicate a structurally unsound building?
- dirt and dust lines along a roof may mean there's a faulty drainage system?
- a shortage of outlets or wall switches could lead to a long, messy, and expensive rewiring process?
- you can gauge the age and efficiency of the plumbing lines by the water pressure and drainage in the tub?

BEFORE YOU BUY YOUR HOUSE OR APARTMENT will answer all your questions—and make sure you live on solid ground for many years to come.

WILLIAM J. KLEIN has been a home inspector since 1965 and has had his own New York City–based inspection business since 1972. His building inspections have covered everything from farmhouses in upstate New York to suburban homes on Long Island, to the condos, town houses, and hundred-unit apartment towers of Manhattan.

BEFORE YOU BUY YOUR HOUSE OR APARTMENT

William J. Klein

WARNER BOOKS

A Warner Communications Company

Copyright © 1987 by William J. Klein
All rights reserved.
Warner Books, Inc., 666 Fifth Avenue, New York, NY 10103

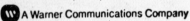 A Warner Communications Company

Printed in the United States of America

First Printing: June 1987

10 9 8 7 6 5 4 3 2 1

Book design: H. Roberts Design
Illustrations: Howard Roberts
Cover Design: Don Puckey

Library of Congress Cataloging-in-Publication Data
Klein, William J.
   Before you buy your house or apartment.

   Includes index.
   1. Dwellings—Inspection.   2. House buying.
3. Apartments—Purchasing.   I. Title.
TH4817.5.K57 1987   643'.12   86-32475
 ISBN 0-446-38434-8 (U.S.A.) (pbk.)

 ISBN 0-446-433-X (Canada) (pbk.)

To Shirley and Noah,
who are most important of all.

CONTENTS _____

INTRODUCTION _____

Buying a house or apartment will probably be one of the most expensive undertakings during your lifetime; it can be a rewarding endeavor with occasional problems, or it can be an ongoing, draining expense with nothing to recommend it on the plus side. If you can head off a potential problem or avoid a troublesome house or apartment altogether, then this book will have accomplished its purpose.

This book uses simple, everyday language. It is a layperson's guide to purchasing a home and will enable you, the prospective buyer, to make a wiser, more informed decision, thus eliminating the need for a purely emotional response when choosing a house or apartment.

Because there are so many facets of a building and so much to look for, I would recommend that after you have finally made a choice, based on this guide and your best judgment, that you then avail yourself of a professional building inspection service. This book should help you avoid the expense of an ill-advised beginning.

BEFORE YOU BUY YOUR HOUSE OR APARTMENT

I.
The
Exterior

There are varied ages and styles of homes that change considerably according to location throughout the country. Certain aspects, like extra insulation, may have little importance in the southern regions. Opened or screened porches will be used infrequently in northern regions. Problems concerning low water tables, underground streams, or flooding conditions are relevant everywhere.

The location of the building in question will affect overall factors. For example, the usual suburban property will be a detached building with space all around it. One side may have a driveway to either an open area, a carport, or a garage. It may be a building that shares a common party wall with another building, which may be a totally separate and different dwelling. If there is a garage, it may be detached, or part of the main building. Some also provide access to the building from inside the parking area.

The urban house will usually be a row house sharing common party walls with adjacent buildings. Normally there will be no garage and little, if any, planted area in front. There could be a plot of land in the rear, which is the width of the building and of varying length, depending on the physical location of the building.

Both urban and suburban housing will have some aspects that are common to both.

Sidewalks

In an urban area there will normally be a sidewalk. It is yours to maintain but may belong to the city, town, or municipality in which the building is located. If the sidewalk is concrete, is it cracked? Are there holes or raised areas? Check for any condition other than smooth, good repair. You will have to maintain the sidewalk to prevent a pedestrian accident, which could result in a liability action.

If the sidewalk is slate or bluestone, are the large blocks level or are there raised or depressed seams that can cause an accident should a pedestrian trip and fall? Leveling heavy slates is an expensive repair job, as is the replacement of a sidewalk. You might consider getting the seller to do the necessary repair work as part of the negotiations for the building.

In addition to concrete, bluestone, and slate, sidewalks can be brick, smooth concrete, or concrete with added pebbles for texture. In a more rural setting, other variations could be gravel, bark chips, or any number of combinations of the aforementioned elements.

Heaved-up walks that are not level, eroded elements, and walks that are mossy or green-stained would be indications of possible drainage problems and/or faulty installation.

Gates

In many cases, older urban houses have iron gates and fences around the front. The oldest buildings have cast-iron fences, posts, and support elements. In Victorian era buildings, handrails, newel posts, and balustrades may also be cast iron. Much of the ironwork was made in sections and bolted together: you should check for separation between pieces, where connecting bolts have rusted away. It is difficult to have cast iron repaired, since most welders do not like to work with it. Internal holes in cast iron have been known to explode when welded.

Rails

Often thin rail covers are rusted through. Look for badly patched ironwork and sections that are held in place with wire or other temporary repairs. You may have to replace most or all of the older iron.

The rear of the urban house may have a patio or an area directly behind the building that is cemented over or paved with bluestone or slate. There should be about three feet directly behind the building where the ground is covered with some solid material, and it should be pitched slightly to the rear of the property: this is nominal assurance that rainwater will run back and away from the building and not seep into a cellar or basement.

Fences

Which fence belongs to whom? In an urban situation, in addition to sharing party walls in a building, you also share fences between properties, whereas in a suburban setting the fence may be a hedge or other type of planting and might tend not to be as clearly defined as a city fence line. Normally, in any fenced situation, adjacent properties share the cost and maintenance of fences, but if you cannot agree on a type or style, you may find that you have to replace one or more fences by yourself.

Fences come in many different types and materials, but you should be looking at condition more than anything else. In wood fencing, check the lower ends of boards or slats where they come into contact with the ground. Check the condition of wood fence posts. You are looking for rot damage or insect infestation. Poking along the lower edge of boards or posts with a screwdriver will give some indication of how solid the wood is.

Backyard

Urban houses usually have a drain at the rear of the building that may or may not go into the main sewer system of the building. If there is one, look it over carefully for rust streaks, cracks, or opened seams.

Depending on the style of row house, there may be an area at the rear of the building where the lower floor is partly below lot grade level but still can be legally occupied. (Usually levels below curb grade cannot be used as living quarters: this may vary according to local building codes.)

"English Basement"

The below-lot grade area is sometimes referred to as an English basement. The rear part of this lower level may contain a kitchen or may have once been a laundry area. There is usually a door or gate from this rear lower room to the garden or rear yard. There should be some type of drain around the rear stairs or in the yard around the back of the wall at the rear of the building. The drain usually goes to the house sewer but may go to a dry well. If there is no drain at the rear area, you may find that there is a problem with flooding or leaking to the rear wall or floor in the rear room.

If you come across this type of rear basement situation, look for damp spots or stains on the rear

and rear-side interior walls. Look for soft or deterio-
rating walls. Check for spongy-feeling walls or floors.
In situations where there has been a long history of
seepage or leaking, there will be a decidedly damp,
musty smell, or mildew on wall or ceiling sections.
Any wet, dark area is also a termite heaven.

The Front Yard

When viewing a suburban building, several aspects
will differ from the inner-city property. There may
or may not be a sidewalk. If there is, its maintenace
or repair will be the same as for the city setting. In
the absence of a sidewalk, a lawn or planted area will
extend down to the curb.

As you first approach the property, notice whether the lawn slopes slightly to the street. This slope
will facilitate the runoff of heavy rains, rather than
depending totally on seepage into the ground for
total drainage. This sloping rule applies also to side
and rear ground or planted areas. Driveways and
walks should also be pitched slightly away from the
house. If there is a driveway on the property, the
best surfaces are concrete or blacktop. Gravel, pebbles, or compacted earth can be a problem in areas
that receive snow. Snow removal can damage substantial portions of these types of surfaces, which, of
course, means that the driveway will need a good
deal of repair, or even partial replacement, in the
spring.

Driveway

If the driveway is concrete, you should look for cracks, depressed or broken areas, and sections where the concrete may have heaved up or lifted. Cracks can be caused by weathering and age. If the driveway is fairly level and in otherwise good condition, cracks can be filled fairly simply.

If there are badly broken or missing sections of cement, heaved-up or depressed areas, then possibly all or part of the driveway will need to be replaced, and with a deeper or more substantial foundation.

A blacktop driveway should be smooth and free of holes and cracks—small cracks or depressed sections can be filled with a cold patch designed for this type of driveway. Driveway sealers or blacktop dressings will usually fill small, thin cracks. If there are deep holes or deeply depressed sections, large cracks, or missing sections, the entire driveway will have to be resurfaced, and possibly sections dug out and replaced.

All driveways, while they should be level and smooth, should also be slightly "crowned": pitched away from the building and sloping toward the street—again to allow for drainage and runoff.

Driveways on steep angles that pitch down from a street to the garage or parking area should have some provision for proper drainage. There should be a grating wide enough and with large enough spaces so it will not fill up with leaves. The grate should drain into a sewer or a dry well. This is essential to prevent water from running down the driveway hill, getting into the garage itself, and possibly into the building. Water that pools around a garage door because of a blocked or faulty drain can freeze in the winter and literally "weld" the door shut.

Brick Walls

Both the urban or suburban house might be of brick construction, and if so, there are specific items to look for in the brickwork itself. Look with particular attention to large, flat areas of brickwork. Important things to look for: Does the brick follow a flat plane?

Shifted brick which may appear in any brick surface.

Are there wavy or bulging sections? Are there bricks that show an obvious shift? These would show up as zigzag lines or cracks through the brick face and look much like a set of stairs as seen from a side view.

Bulging or otherwise shifted brick might show up as rounded areas that do not appear to be flat within a flat surface. If you can reach a suspected area of bulging brickwork, tap it with a hard implement (a screwdriver handle, for example). If this produces a hollow sound, different from the sound heard when a flatter area is tapped, it is a possible indication of brick face that has separated or lost its bond with the underlying support structure.

The material beneath the brick face may also be brick or could be another type of rigid material, such as concrete or cinder blocks, or possibly a poured concrete wall. In any case, the hollow sound in company with the bulging brick will probably mean that some of the brick will have to be removed and reset so that it is tightly fastened to the substructure. Bulging or cracked brick will allow water to seep in under the brick face and can freeze and destroy the brick. Seepage through the wall to the inside of the building can damage walls and ceilings.

Another aspect of the brick that should be checked carefully is the brick pointing: the mortar joints between bricks. Look for uneven, extra wide joints running vertically at the corner edges of the building: This might be another indication of the shifting of brick face. Carefully check front-to-side and/or rear-to-side corners where possible (this may be impossible in an attached row house). Look for missing mortar or loose and uneven joints. Any of these conditions could mean an expensive repointing job.

A brick face or a partial wall section of brick is sometimes merely a thin brick veneer fastened to the actual structural wall of a building. This is more typical in suburban settings and is installed as a decorative accent, though it may be used anywhere as a covering material. If there is any cracking, bulging, or shifting in a brick veneer wall, there can be serious problems with the actual structure or foundation wall of the building itself. These problems show up on the interior walls behind the exterior problem area. There may be visible mildew, deteriorated plaster, or a damp, clammy feel to the wall.

In some instances a brick or stone wall looks so perfect that on closer inspection it will reveal itself to be something else again. It will probably be cement-cut or shaped to look like either brick or stone. This is achieved by fastening a heavy metal grid or wire lath to the exterior of the building, covering this with a cement coating, and applying a second cement coating in a contrasting color over the first one. The top coat is then cut, carved, or otherwise shaped to look like brick or stone. A similar facing is also put up in sections that are fastened directly to the original exterior walls. This is not as convincing as the cut cement. The seams may be more noticeable, since the brick or stone pattern repeats regularly like wallpaper.

The exterior of a building can be covered with many different materials: asphalt shingles, asbestos shingles, aluminum or wood siding, stucco, stone, and probably half a dozen other materials or combinations.

Brownstone Walls

In older, inner-city communities, brownstone is the commonest material used. Brownstone is a relatively soft material, is easy to work and carve, and is used extensively because of its economy. If you are interested in a brownstone building, some of the things to look for are: surface cracks; bulged or raised sections of stonework; spalling or partly rotted and/or deteriorated stone. Check for erosion of carved detail work and missing stone, where deterioration has caused sections of stone to fall.

To re-create its original look, the restoration of a brownstone front can be a very costly process. All loose or deteriorated stone would have to be chiseled back to a sound surface and then the entire front refaced with brownstone-colored cement. Sills, lintels, and other details have to be hand-shaped or built up with wood forms. In the process of restoring or facing an entire front, a good deal of high-relief, ornate detail is lost and not recopied. Extreme detail is very expensive to reproduce, and to do so a mason might have to resort to rubber molds or other casting processes. Since most stonemasons are less than creative, the ornate detail is usually replaced with much simpler designs.

A less costly restoration to a brownstone front would be the replacement of the deteriorated stonework with cement. This cement requires painting, which means repainting the entire building face. The painted surface will have to be renewed periodically. The time elapsing between paint jobs will depend upon the type of paint used, weather, and pollution conditions. One problem with the repair and paint process is that some loose or questionable stone will probably be left, and this, in time, will start to flake away. A mason is likely to leave alone an area that looks sound rather than test its quality.

The rear face of an urban brownstone or brick building would normally be brick, as would the side walls; in an attached row of buildings the sidewalls would not be accessible, except for buildings at the end of a row or corner properties.

Roof Drains

Looking over the rear face, special attention should be paid to the condition of mortar joints (pointing), where cement may have washed out. Missing cement will need to be replaced. Many buildings have rear drainpipes coming from the roof. Water can leak through drains, whose age and wear leave them cracked, rusty, and/or with holes or separated seams. A large volume of water coming off the roof and spraying through holes or cracks in a drain hits the wall with a good deal of pressure and quickly erodes the mortar in brick joints. A drainpipe in even questionable condition will need to be replaced. Brickwork along the line of drains, therefore, should be carefully checked. Pointing of brick can be very expensive if there is a considerable amount that needs to be done. Loose joints have to be chiseled out, cleaned, checked, and then the cement has to be replaced by hand, using thin trowels and pointing tools. When the mortar is nearly set, a jointer is run over the cement to correct the shape or type of joint. All this hand labor would be appropriate to the front of a building, but for the back it might be considered an excessive expense.

A less costly alternate to pointing a rear wall would be to have the entire back cemented over. This would fill the defective joints, but of course also puts cement over the brick surfaces. While it might not be as aesthetically pleasing, it waterproofs the rear of the building. There are pigmented concrete coatings that are available. To be brushed on, they dry in thinner layers.

Limestone

Another common material used in older urban housing is limestone: it is a harder and denser material than brownstone and normally does not suffer from the same problems of deterioration. When checking a limestone building, you will be looking for stone deterioration, but you should also be looking for separations between stone blocks where mortar has washed out. Large gaps between stone blocks are areas where rain can seep into the building and affect interior walls or ceilings.

These gaps can be a major problem during severe winters. Water can freeze and cause stones to crack as ice expands; as the cracks get larger, more water can get in, and the problem compounds itself. Outside stone sills and lintels should be checked for broken or missing parts—often gaps develop where they are set into the building face. Because mortar joints at the junction are not tightly sealed, water gets in, causes cracking, and again, stone deterioration.

Wood

Both urban and suburban housing share a common material: wood. The use of wood was determined by availability and relative expense as opposed to the cost of transporting stone or brick over long distances. Some of the oldest wood and wood-framed buildings used brick between interior studding—not exterior quality brick but dried brick rather than hard-fired. If there was no easily available stone and no refractory, then wood was used.

The wood used for urban housing might be whatever was most available in the locality of the building site. Often a wood lot was cleared, lumber sawed on the spot, and then stored until the foundations were dug for a block of houses. By that time the wood was dry enough to use.

The type of wood used is not very important, since it was all to be painted anyway, and so you might start by examining the condition of the paint. The painted surface should be smooth and of a uniform color with no visible streaks or blotches.

Look for blistered or bubbled areas, or areas where the paint has peeled. Any of these problems might indicate an area where moisture has penetrated into the wood under the paint and lifted the paint off.

Blisters also show up where the original wood was stained and then painted. This might be an indication of wood that was not sealed over the stain prior to painting. Or it could indicate an incompatible primer used under the finishing coat. Blisters and bubbled areas will have to be sanded down to the wood and a new primer applied.

After the primer dries, a new finishing coat will have to be applied to match the rest of the painted areas. If there are many blistered or bubbled sections, you may have to repaint all the woodwork. Check carefully, since a new paint job can be an expensive addition to a new home.

All exterior wood should be checked for broken or missing trim or moldings. Look for cracks or gaps where wood sections are built up or joined. Check carefully for obvious deterioration that might be rot or termite- or other insect-caused injury.

Exterior wood stairs and stairs connected to porches or balconies should be checked for rigidity. How level are they in relation to other horizontal sections of the building? The condition of the wood should be checked. If there is any suspicion of rot or other damage, try poking that area with your screwdriver.

Extended parts of wood buildings, such as bay windows, should be checked carefully for vertical plumb with the main building. You should also look carefully for gaps or openings where a bay window meets the building. Look for tilted or sagged wood members, anything that is not level or plumb. Any gaps or tilting might indicate that a bay or other part of the structure is falling off the main building. It may also mean that the wall of the building is pulling away.

The exterior materials used in suburban housing varies much more than in urban dwellings. The

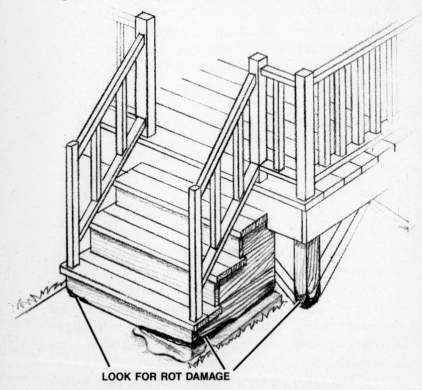

LOOK FOR ROT DAMAGE

Exterior wood stairs can develop rot problems where wood contacts ground.

design of buildings and the material used in a particular design type varies to some extent by geographi-
cal location.

The choice of building materials will also vary to
some degree within a specific area, depending on
when the building was built and what the dominant
building style was at the time. Styles and materials
also vary within an area because of a builder's or
developer's design. Different styles occur when homes
were not built in large tract developments but by
smaller builders. There may be buildings mixed in
that were built to an owner's specifications or where
construction costs allowed for various styles and types
of housing within a price range. The costs of development and construction in recent years do not
allow for much individual design, except for very
expensive custom housing.

Wood Exterior

Tract or row housing, using the same basic plan with
minor trim changes, can be put up on very nearly an
assembly line basis. In rural or suburban settings you
may find wood buildings that have been stained
rather than painted, or left unfinished to weather.
The exterior wood might be shingles, shakes, or
siding. A sealer may or may not have been applied.
You may also find buildings covered with tongue-and-
groove boards or wood panels with battens over
seams.

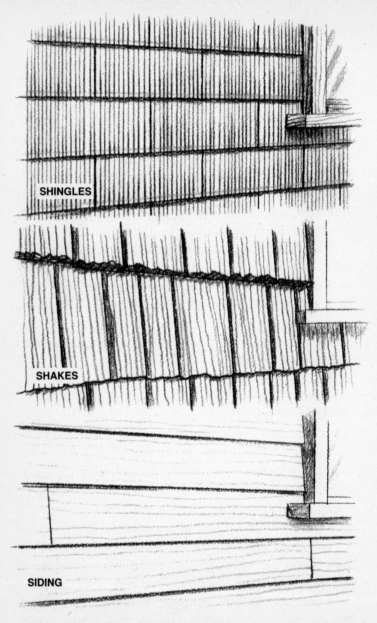

SHINGLES

SHAKES

SIDING

The most common suburban exteriors are shingles, shakes, or some type of siding.

Regardless of the type of wood and the design or application, the main concern should be its condition. Look for broken or missing shingles. Look for wood that has obvious rot or other damage. Any wood that runs close to the ground should be checked carefully for rot damage or insect infestation. Wood that is close to the ground can soak up water if snow lies against it.

Lifted, rough, warped, or raised shingles or wood members can be indicators of water damage. Exterior painted surfaces should also be checked as previously outlined.

Siding or plank exterior walls should be checked for cracking or large gaps and raised or missing sections of wood.

Asbestos Shingles

Exterior asbestos shingles are fairly brittle, and any building covered with them should be looked at carefully for broken, cracked, or missing sections. If the shingles are old, it may be difficult to match a color or pattern needed for replacements. Rust or water streaks on exterior walls should be traced back to their source: They can indicate cracked or otherwise defective drain gutters or leaders.

Asphalt Shingles

Asphalt shingles are another common exterior surface covering that may be found anywhere in the country. Worn areas tend to show up as dull places where the original color has worn away. Asphalt shingles have a "glitter" coat that wears away with time. A dull, faded color is usually an indication of age. Very dark areas reveal the black backing of shingles showing through. Broken or missing shingles, in addition to extensive wear and deterioration, will probably mean that the wall and possibly the entire building will need to be recovered. One wall can be recovered at a time, but you may find it is impossible to match a color or even a shape later on.

Aluminum Siding

Aluminum siding is another fairly common exterior covering that you may find almost anywhere, although it is probably more common in a suburban area. If aluminum siding is correctly installed, it should fit very neatly around doors and windows and have no gaps or openings at corners. Aluminum siding comes with a baked-on finish. Look for cracked or abraded areas along the surface. In checking over the entire building, you should look for lifted or loose corners and any area that does not lie in a flat plane.

Aluminum siding that does not have breather holes can cause rot damage to wood buildings because of condensation between the siding and the original exterior wall of the building. A building that is heated in winter will lose a certain amount of heat through the exterior walls. Exterior metal siding exposed to the weather is very cold, and so the heated air, on contact with the metal, forms water droplets; if there are no breather holes, the water runs back into the wood of the building and, because it cannot evaporate, causes a rotting problem.

Plastic or vinyl siding should be checked as for aluminum. They look alike, but plastic gives when pressed and has no metallic sound when tapped.

Exterior Brick and Stone

Combinations of brick and stone are not uncommon. You should check the fitting of one to the other. The fitting also should be carefully checked in all stone buildings where rough or uncut stone is used. Mortar joints should be checked for the condition of the cement, joints should be tight, and the pointing or cement fill should be smooth. Look for stone that has shifted or bulged outward. Look for any part of the wall where stone and/or brick has created a pocket that will allow water to stand and possibly seep into the inner walls of the building. Water that sits in small pools in low areas of a stone wall can become a mosquito hatchery.

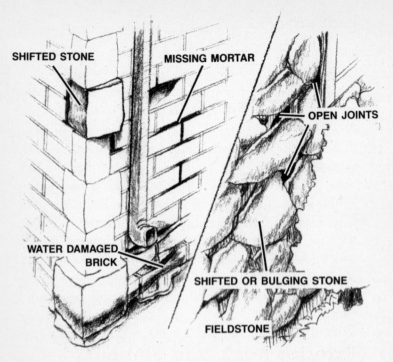

Check combination of brick and stone for fit and condition.

Badly eroded stone or brick can be caused by a continuous flow of water over that particular section of wall when it rains. Look for rain gutters over a bad spot in a wall and try to determine if the gutter is leaking or has an opened seam. Look for a leader (drain) connection from a gutter that may not fit tightly or may have a crack or hole. Also examine roof, porch, or other overhangs.

Stucco Exterior

Combinations of stucco, stone, wood, and brick are very popular building materials in the suburbs.

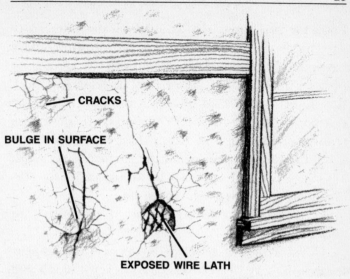

CRACKS

BULGE IN SURFACE

EXPOSED WIRE LATH

Stucco may develop cracks over a winter as the building expands and contracts.

Stucco is a finish that is normally installed over wood-frame construction but may be used for trim or detailing in any other type of building.

Stucco is achieved by nailing a heavy wire lath or mesh grill over a water-resistant building paper, over which cement is troweled in two or three applications. The finished coat may be smooth or textured and may be colored prior to application. It can also be painted or left its natural color.

Things to look for are: cracks larger than a hairline; bulging or raised areas not level with the surrounding plane; and missing sections. Any of these conditions can indicate a problem with the wire lath or the basic wood structure of the building. Rusted or deteriorated wire lath can cause the cement to come away from the building in large pieces.

Look for rust stains that could indicate water seepage under the stucco. If you check carefully above rust stains, you may find openings in the cement or places where a drain gutter may be leaking. Check for deteriorated and spalling cement. Look for discolored or mismatched cement, both in surface texture or in design of finish. Large patched areas should be questioned: when the surface is very old, any large patched area can be an indication of surface material failure, which can be the beginning of other repairs, or possibly the need to replace an entire wall.

Most types of exterior materials that appear frequently have been covered, and even though you may find other types or mixtures of materials, the points covered should be relevant to any other facade you may encounter. These points concerning exterior finishes apply also to detached garages and other outbuildings.

Garages

Check garage doors for fit and ease of operation. If the doors are hinged, swing them open all the way to see if hinges are firmly set and to make sure the door or doors clear the driveway and do not drag on the ground. Door locks should be checked, as should all hardware that holds doors in place.

Rolling doors should be checked for ease of operation. Also make sure rollers turn and do not just slide. Check for very rusty rollers or tracks. Roll-up doors should be opened and closed to see that they operate freely. Look along the door face for broken or split sections, and check cables, springs, and tracks for heavy rust buildup. Electrically operated doors should be tried with the interior switch, the outside key switch, and the electronic sensor if there is one.

While in the garage, look over the floor area, checking for cracked or broken concrete and for raised or heaved-up areas, which could be indicators of groundwater coming up into the garage. Look at the ceiling and check for wet spots or stains, which would indicate a leaking roof. Dry stains could indicate an old, repaired leak; the staining can be accompanied by rot damage to wood sections, so look for powdery or flaking wood.

Structural or support walls should be gone over for cracking or shifting. Internal garage walls of concrete or cinder block sometimes show structural cracks that have been covered on the outside. Cracks that show through patched areas are indicators of continual movement and should be thoroughly investigated.

Insect or Rot Damage

Exposed wood beams or joists should be carefully checked for termite or other insect damage: wood that is in close contact with damp earth is a natural

Any untreated exterior wood, such as fences and posts, may develop rot or insect damage.

target for insects and is also highly susceptible to rotting problems. Exterior wood framing and other wood trim should be carefully inspected for soft, spongy wood and sawdust, which would indicate some gnawing action. Carpenter ants and boring bees leave sawdust. Look for the destroyed ends of boards and framing.

While still on the outside of the building, you should pay some attention to the windows, which for some reason are often overlooked by buyers and home inspectors. One obvious thing to look for is broken or missing glass. Glass is inexpensive, but the cost for broken window replacement can be sizable, especially if a glazier has to work on a high ladder.

Windows

Windows should also be checked from inside the house for fit and ease of operation. Loosely fitting windows are not weather-tight. An ill-fitting or badly shrunken wood sash will not go up or down without binding.

If the building has storm sashes, normally they will be on the outside of older windows. Storm window frames should fit tightly where the outer frames are fastened to the building, regardless of building material used for construction. Storm window frames should also be caulked along the edges where they fit into or around window frames or openings. Look for gaps, cracks, and missing caulking: Any area that is not tightly filled is a potential leak source, either into the building or along the edges of older framing material. Leaking around a storm sash is a potential window frame rot problem. It could also lead to water damage of internal walls and ceilings.

The condition of the putty that holds glass in frames is often overlooked. Missing putty can permit glass to shift or fall and will also allow wood frames to rot. Missing putty in steel casement units creates rusting problems.

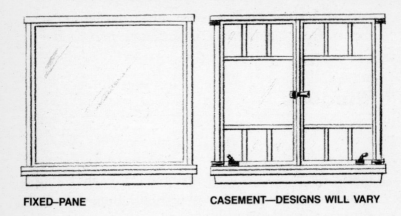

FIXED–PANE   **CASEMENT—DESIGNS WILL VARY**

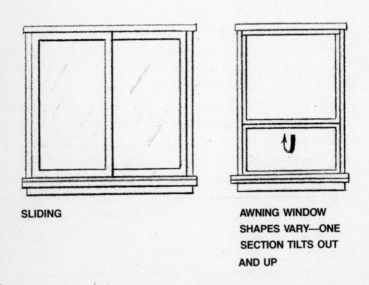

SLIDING   **AWNING WINDOW
SHAPES VARY—ONE
SECTION TILTS OUT
AND UP**

Typical windows.

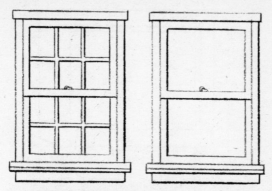

DOUBLE HUNG WINDOWS MAY HAVE CHAINS, ROPE OR SPRING BALANCERS

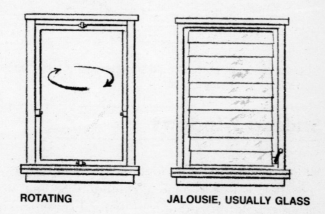

ROTATING   **JALOUSIE, USUALLY GLASS**

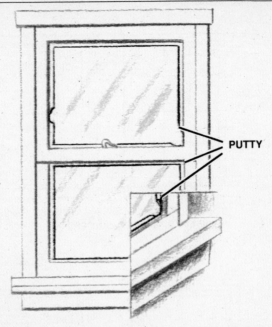

PUTTY

The condition of putty should be checked in all windows, as well as in cracked glass.

Sliding Windows

Sliding wood windows should be checked for ease of operation as well as general condition. Sliding metal sashes should, in addition to general condition and ease of operation, be checked for pitting and corrosion.

If windows have been factory-finished, some attention should be paid to the condition of the surface. Depending upon the type of window, the finish could be a baked enamel; an anodized finish on aluminum; or a vinyl surface on wood.

Metal Casement Windows

Metal casement windows should fit tightly and have no gaps at the points where they fit into their frames; look for rusted spots or places where metal has rusted through.

All hardware, including latches and other closures, should be tried on all doors and windows. On double-hung sashes (the type where one goes up and one down) there is usually a center catch where the two half windows meet. This catch should be in line and, when closed, pull the other two parts of the window (upper and lower) together slightly. On newer double-hung units there may be a groove or spline that fits the two halves tightly.

In older buildings double-hung windows are operated with weights and rope (sash cord). The rope runs over a pulley and as the window is raised, the weight lowers into a sash pocket. Because the window and the weight weigh the same, the window would stay wherever it was stopped. As time goes by, the ropes wear and need to be replaced with sash chain. After a period of time rope was eliminated altogether, but there are still many windows in older buildings that have rope. If you come across windows like this, you can anticipate having to replace them. For some reason there is a rule that says the rope will break as soon as the window has been painted.

Double-hung Windows

Old sash chains and pulleys should be clean. Heavily encrusted paint on the chain or the pulley will have to be removed, and you should anticipate the work that will have to be done. If you find windows with broken or disconnected chains or ropes, the chances are good that the pulley is painted in and cannot roll: this makes the sash weight bounce and snaps the cord or chain.

Newer double-hung sashes operate with spring balancers and eliminate the need for weights and chains. Metal-lined channels and no visible chains or pulleys indicate the new type of window.

Front Door

The entrance, be it an iron gate on an old urban brownstone; a modern sliding glass patio door; an aluminum storm door; or any other type of door, should first be checked for fit. Does the door bind at the top or bottom? Does it stick along any of the edges or does it drag at the bottom over a saddle? Many times doors that drag or bind do so because hinges have come loose or doors or frames have warped. Sliding doors should be checked to see that they move smoothly.

Door hardware should be tried for fit and should operate smoothly without being forced; locks, latches, and other closures should be free and not bind.

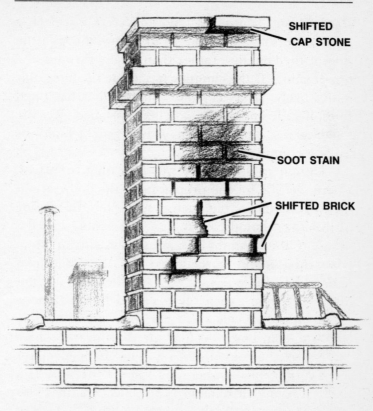

SHIFTED
CAP STONE

SOOT STAIN

SHIFTED BRICK

Typical chimney problems are shifted or broken brick, missing mortar, or soot stains.

Chimneys

Chimneys that cannot be reached from a roof can be checked from ground level using a pair of binoculars. You will not be able to get to the top of the chimney, but you can look over mortar joints and see if there are any shifted or displaced bricks or stones.

Dark or sooty stains may indicate a crack or opening in the flue that allows smoke to escape through the side of the chimney, rather than totally through the top opening. If the chimney has a flue tile liner, this is not likely. In a very old building that has lined flues, the tile liners may have been installed after the building was built and put in to repair a faulty or leaking chimney.

In buildings that have wood-burning fireplaces, where the flue for the fireplace and the boiler are in the same chimney but each is separately flued, one of the units should have a higher elevation than the other. If the chimney has more than two or three flues, they should be staggered and alternated: one higher than the one next to it. If the flues are not different heights, then there should be separations or dividers between them. If flues are the same height and in line, you may get downdrafts, which can cause a smoky fireplace. This happens most often if the boiler is operating when a fire is lit. If a flue is dirty or the damper is defective, you may also get smoke coming back into the building

Chimneys should have screens over the top to keep leaves, squirrels, and the occasional bird out.

Flat Roofs

Roofs come in various styles, shapes, and material types. Urban housing is likely to have flat, rolled roofing. To judge the condition of a flat roof, it helps to know how it was installed. Normally the paper is laid out and cemented down so that one strip overlaps the previous one, with the overlap occurring in the direction that the roof will drain. This overlap permits water to run over the seams rather than under them. Flat roofs pitch slightly toward a drain. The drain is usually at the back of the building but can be in the front or on the side

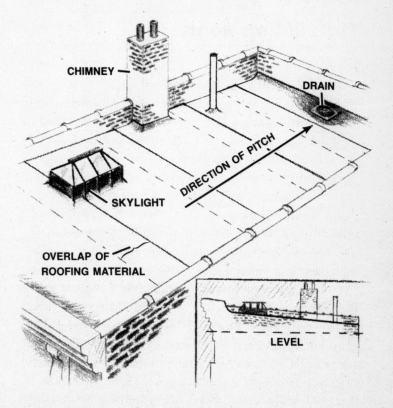

CHIMNEY

DRAIN

DIRECTION OF PITCH

SKYLIGHT

OVERLAP OF ROOFING MATERIAL

LEVEL

Typical flat roof.

and sometimes occurs in the center of the roof, in which case the roof will pitch to the center in four directions.

Roofing paper is installed from side to side; if you come across a roof where the paper has been installed from front to rear with an overlap, you can be nearly certain that the roof will leak.

Flat, Rolled Roofs

Sometimes a flat, rolled roof is installed with the paper butted edge to edge rather than overlapped. This would be a double roof: the paper is installed in long lengths from front to back, butted one strip to the other, and then another roof put over it running from side to side and also butted edge to edge. The paper will appear as full width in this type of installation. If you find a roof of this type, you should question the owner and, if possible, see the bill for installation, otherwise you may find that it is incorrectly installed with only single-width paper.

A paper roof surface usually has a slightly gritty or reflective coating when it is new—this dulls down as the roof ages. Worn or blotchy areas are indications of the beginning of surface deterioration. Flat roofs with reasonable surface wear should not be rejected as needing replacement. Holes or cracks in the roof surface, however, are potential, or possibly active, leak sources.

Most flat roofs have parapets running around

the roof perimeter. Attached buildings also have a low parapet between roofs, following the line of the party walls. Flashing on a roof is the covering on the sweep upward from the roof and running vertically to either the top of the parapet or up to a cap or coping. Many times the flashing has hollow sections because of the curve, and the hollows crack through or develop holes. This is very common, especially in the area around chimneys. These openings produce leaking problems to the ceiling on the floor below the roof. The leak marks will show up where the ceiling and wall meet. On a flat roof you may find bubbled areas, where air is trapped between the roof boards and the covering. If the roof is not walked on and the bubbles do not become pierced, then the bubbles usually will not cause a problem. Light foot pressure on a bubbled area will show whether it is holding air: pressure causes air to be expelled, which indicates a hole in the bubble and signals the need for a patching job.

Applied pressure on a bubbled or raised area of roofing will sometimes cause water to seep or squirt out of a hole or along a seam. This is water that is trapped between the roof surface and the roof boards, and it will soon find its way into the building and affect ceilings or walls on the floor below. Trapped water can be released by opening the area around the water exit, drying the roofing under the opened bubble, refastening the roofing paper, and patching the cut. Look carefully: Roof repairs are not one of the first things you will want to do when moving into a new home.

Pebble Roofs

Occasionally you will find a pebble-covered roof, many of which are fifty years old. Originally these roofs had hot tar poured over them, and then pebbles were scattered over the tar surface to reflect heat. This type of roof now presents several problems: one is that many years of soot and dust build-up causes rainwater to pool, rather than run off.

Old pebble roofs also hold water in winter, which, when it freezes, cracks the tar base and can allow seepage into the building. Since pebbles have to be scraped away to find leak sources, repairs are difficult, and you can anticipate having to replace this type of roof almost immediately. If you are planning to do any ceiling repairs or painting on the floor below a tar-and-pebble roof, the roof should be done as part of the plan and done first.

Although urban roofing is usually flat, shingle-covered pitched roofs do exist. If accessible, the roof should be inspected close-up. If it has to be seen from street level, binoculars will help. Shingled roofing suffers from the same problems as shingle siding; more exposure to the elements, though, usually causes faster wear and damage.

Roofs may have ornate setbacks, built-up sections, or ornate design elements. Roofs may be slate, tile, or a combination of materials. If you look long enough, you may find copper, lead, or steel. Wood shingles are not uncommon. Despite the variety of materials, there are very similar problems to look for.

Look at your roof carefully for missing, lifted, or displaced parts. Surface condition should be observed, as should the fit of various joints, valleys, and hips. How well do the gutters, leaders, and other drain elements fit? Special attention should be paid to roofing where there are elaborate design elements and setbacks, which also contain, or are, the drain gutters for the building. Any gutter that is pitched incorrectly will present a potential leakage problem. On flat roofs where the pitch is incorrect, you will find areas where water has not run off through a drain and has pooled at the drain area or at some other lower section of roof. If the roof is dry, you can sometimes discover where the water pools by looking for a slightly different color on the surface paper. Often you will see dirt, dust, or other deposits on the roof surface that represent "tidelines."

Any roof that has a pitch problem also has a potential leakage problem. Low spots or incorrectly pitched areas should be checked periodically and probably should be sealed or coated from time to time as insurance against leakage. A flat roof may have to be built up slightly to correct a pitch or drainage problem.

Roofing in the Pacific Northwest or other areas where there is a lot of rain or moisture develops a heavy moss buildup. This is also an indication of poor drainage. If the moss is not removed every so often, the moisture held by it will cause rot damage to the roof; as the moss size and area increases it will get under shingles and lift or break them.

On a flat roof you should have access to a close

visual examination of chimneys. Look at the condition of the brick pointing. Check to see if the chimneys are plumb. Look for tilting or shifting and also check for missing or broken brick.

At least one, and possibly two, flues will probably be used for a hot water tank or central heating plant. Other flues not being used for fireplaces should be capped to retain heat within the building.

Many of the flues in older urban buildings are not lined for wood-burning fireplaces. A lot of them were used for gas fires, or for soft coal, where the flue was intended mainly to take fumes out and to provide a draft. A wood fire produces soot, sparks, and a creosotelike coating inside the flue. Where there is no liner, the soot will fill in mortar joints and can cause a chimney fire because of heat and sparks. If you are planning on using a fireplace for wood, it should be checked out by a fireplace specialist before it is used.

Skylights

If there is an accessible skylight, you should examine the condition of the glass and the metal framing that holds the glass in place. Many times the metal frames are covered with tar, and this would indicate that there is little actual metal left. This indicates imminent replacement. Metal skylight frames should be painted to prevent rusting. Occasionally you come across an old copper skylight that can be left unpainted.

Look for holes or cracks around the skylight framing where it fits through the roof. By the way, how did you get to the roof?

Fire Escapes

If it was by a fire escape, did you look at the condition of the paint? Did you look for rusting or loose sections? Were the stairs or handrails loose? Are there any missing bolts or metal parts?

If you got to the roof through a scuttle opening or a trapdoor, was the cover secured? Does the cover fit tightly, and what is its condition? Many older wood covers on flat roofs will be in poor condition. They are also usually very heavy. Since the scuttle is an additional exit from a fire situation, you might consider a more lightweight cover to replace the old one and secure the opening.

Roof Ladders

The original, old wood ladders to roofs are usually not very steady or secure, unless they have been replaced. If access to the roof was via internal stairs and through a bulkhead, then pay close attention to the bulkhead walls and ceiling, especially if there is a skylight. The door to the roof from the bulkhead should be checked carefully for fit and for building security. Since the door to a roof and the scuttle cover act as fire escapes, local building or fire codes may prohibit their being locked. You can check exact requirements in that locality.

A rare find in roofing materials is wood shingles or shakes, because usually these have been replaced with other materials over the years. If you are looking at a building with wood roof shingles, you should be looking for missing, rotted, or warped shingles. Badly discolored wood might indicate a leak from an overhang or a faulty drain gutter. Wet wood is usually followed by rotting problems.

Wood Shingles or Shakes

If a large area of wood shingles needs replacement, you may have to recover the entire roof with another material: many local fire ordinances will not allow wood roofing as a new installation and only allow a certain amount of replacement. Consult the local fire or building department.

Asphalt Shingles

Asphalt and asphalt reinforced with fiberglass shingles look enough alike and are installed in the same way, so that your inspection of either one will be for the same things. It is doubtful if you or anyone else

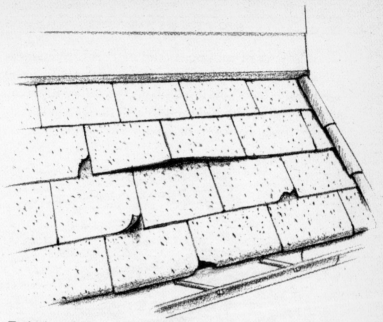

Typical asphalt shingle problems are bent corners, broken corners, lifted or missing pieces.

could tell the difference between the two without reading the label, anyway. Both types of shingles are factory-coated with a gritty mineral surface not unlike coarse sand. The surface glitters slightly when the sun hits it. You will be looking for dull, discolored surfaces or places that look very worn. Look for lifted or broken shingles or where the corners are curled up. Look for clean lines and a smooth fit where corners meet, and also look for a tight fit at the top row where shingles meet a wall, porch, or other offset. At this joint there should be some type of flashing; copper is best, but fiberglass is less expensive and probably more common now.

If the roof is not accessible, or setbacks or porch overhangs cannot be seen up close or through a window, then the binoculars will help.

All types of roofing should be checked for moss growth, green stains, or any other growth. Trapped water will feed low-level plants, such as moss or algae. Small plants and even tree seedlings can sprout on flat roofs via wind- or bird-borne seeds.

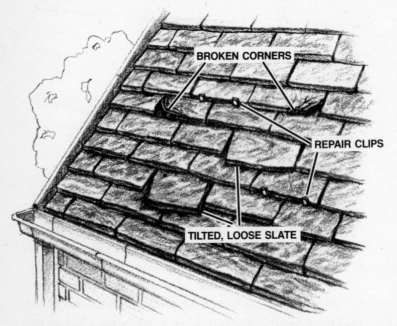

A slate roof may have broken or missing corners, cracks, or shifted slate.

Slate Roofs

Slate roofs are one of the most durable types but realistically do not last forever. Finding a crack in an individual slate is difficult, even if you scrutinized every inch of the roof. Slates naturally have surface cracks and raised sections—neither of these is likely to be a leak source. Pitched-type slate roofs make close inspection virtually impossible. You will probably have to concentrate your search in the attic or crawl space.

You should be looking for missing or broken slates, and slates with large pieces missing. Check carefully for shifted slates that are out of line or tilted. If you follow the pattern of a slate roof going along the horizontal seams, you have a better chance of discovering existing problems. Shifted or replacement slates are often reset and held in place with copper or aluminum clips or angled metal pieces. If there are many of these visible on a roof, you may anticipate other areas of the roof needing repairs in a fairly short time. A good slate roofer (and they are hard to find) should be able to repair and replace with no visible clips.

The original slates were held in place with copper nails, and as one slate overlaps another, starting at the bottom, the nails do not show. For some unknown reason you may at times find a group of buildings built at the same time and possibly by the same builder, all of which have poor slate roofs. The slate looks as though it needs total replacement, and you may see large areas of roofing that have shifted or slid down and sideways. The problem may be poor materials, a defective batch of nails or slate, or poor workmanship. If the building you are looking at is one of such a group and yours has a good roof, you should try to determine if it was repaired or replaced. If not, it may be the next to go.

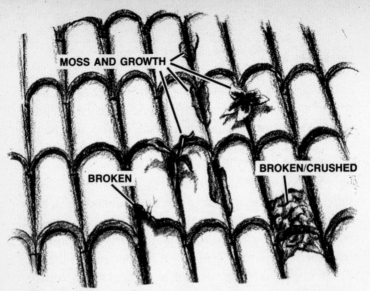

Terra cotta may become cracked, broken or crushed due to its brittle nature.

Roof Tiles

Terra-cotta, or what is commonly known as Spanish tile, is a hard-surfaced material, similar in wearing qualities to slate, but it is a manufactured product and tends to be brittle and will crack with very little surface impact. These tiles are usually a reddish-clay color but may be glazed with nearly any color. As in slate, look for cracked, broken, or missing sections of tile: sometimes one or more will be so badly broken that it appears to be crushed. Look carefully for moss or other growth between the deep convolutions of the design on the tile.

Anything growing on any roof surface can and will allow moisture into the building. Roots will lift tile or slate and can eventually break them.

Gutters

Once again, looking at leaders and gutters: They should be fastened firmly to the building with no gaps and no pulled-away sections, in either the vertical or horizontal planes. Streaks or stains along gutters or leaders will indicate seepage or leaking, especially at joints or seams where sections fit together. There can be streaks along any part of the leader or drain system, and this leaking can be rusted or rotted-through pipe.

Drains

Gutters and leaders may drain off in different ways; the leader might be connected to the house sewer system and run off to a main street sewer. It might end with an elbow on the leader pipe that drains off onto a driveway or along the property line and into the planted area of the building lot. The pitch and grade of the building should be such that water from the drains runs away from the building and not toward it, and especially not toward a cellar window. A leader pipe that runs into the ground either directly or through a lower section of cast iron, clay, or plastic pipe can drain into a dry well.

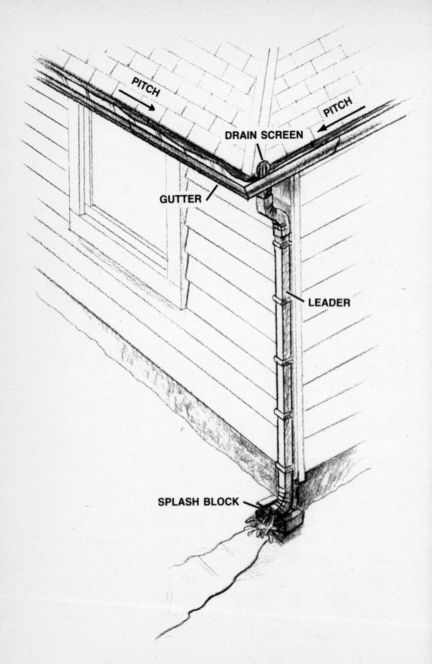

Typical suburban leader and gutter system.

Dry Well

A properly constructed dry well allows water to drain into a type of underground container with many openings, which allows the water to dissipate below the surface. Often dry wells are not what they should be, and the drain leader from the house runs into a subsurface rock pile, rather than a real cement block housing. Short of digging up the yard, not you nor anyone else will be able to tell. Indications of blocked or backed-up dry wells will usually show up on cellar walls and usually directly behind or close to where the leader pipe goes into the ground. Dry wells do get blocked at times because of leaves or

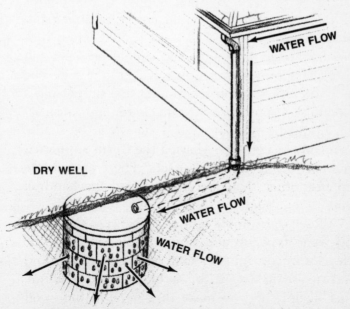

A well-constructed dry well is not just a pile of broken rock.

other debris that gets into the gutters and leaders. If you are looking at a building during a fairly heavy rain and the drains into the ground are visible, look for water "boiling" or "percolating" over the top of the pipe above ground level. That is usually an indication of a blocked dry well. Sometimes you will see water coming up through a lawn in the area of the downspout, and that, too, would be an indicator.

Wood Stairs

Walking around the outside of any building, you should be taking note of exterior stairs. Wood stairs should be checked for their supports. Wood posts are fairly common but should not be in direct contact with the ground. The posts should be on concrete or masonry footings and should be separated from the footings with a metal plate and leg. The same wood-post construction might be supporting a wood deck or porch, so the same lower-end construction would be relevant. Wood stairs can be of the open construction type—having the treads supported on a long stringer with no risers. There are no side supports other than the stringer and the handrail supports or spindles.

Closed stairs would have risers between the treads and some type of side support construction. The side closure or support may go from the ground level up to the treads, or as high as the handrail. Once again, check to make sure none of the wood

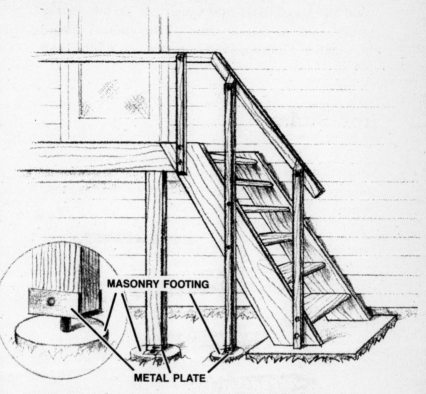

Wood posts should be separated from the ground and on masonry footings.

comes in direct contact with the ground. Exterior wood closed stairs should be built so that rainwater does not collect at the rear corner where risers and treads meet. Holes drilled in treads do not provide a satisfactory remedy and only add to the possibility of rot damage.

Wood stairs and their supports should be painted, stained, or sealed with weatherproof coatings. Red-

wood or pressure-treated wood can be left in the
natural state in certain parts of the country where
the weather conditions are not excessively humid or
damp.

Iron Stairs

Iron stairs, or iron in use with another material,
should be checked for the condition of the fasteners

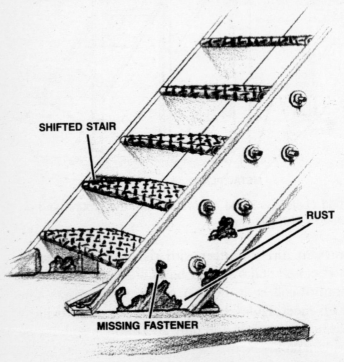

Metal stairs may have missing pieces, rust, peeling paint,
and may be shaky and unstable.

between the iron and the wood, stone, slate, or whatever the other material might be. The iron should be checked for rusting, rough spots, and for sound construction. If iron is welded, joints should be clean and smooth. If bolted, all bolts and nuts should be installed with no opened holes. All metal parts should be rigid and have a solid feel; there should be no shaky feeling when traversed. Metal supports should be on concrete or masonry footings above ground level. Concrete footings should be tapered away from a leg, enabling water to run away from the metal. All ironwork should be painted to prevent rusting. Look over the condition of the paint of any ironwork. If there is a lot of rust, or if rust is appearing through the paint, you will at least have to wire-brush, scrape, and paint; but you also may have to replace one or more sections.

Brick Stairs

Where brick stairs are concerned, you must look at the condition of the bricks themselves to determine if any will need replacement. Broken, rotted, or deteriorated bricks will have to be changed. The brick pointing should be checked for missing or deteriorated mortar. Look for shifted or bulging brick—any bricks that are out of line in a row. Look around the side supports of the stairs for any shifting or settling problems.

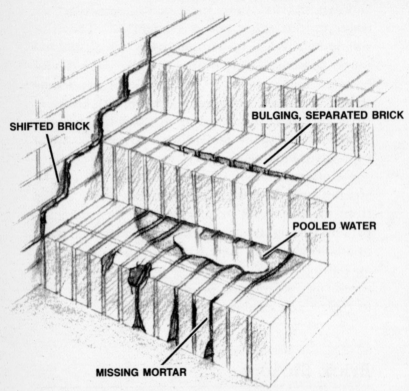

SHIFTED BRICK

BULGING, SEPARATED BRICK

POOLED WATER

MISSING MORTAR

In brick stairs look for separated, shifted, or broken brick.
Where stairs have dropped the footing may be defective.

Stone-in-concrete Stairs

Stair types or styles will vary with the type of building
and its age and location. In a suburban location you
might find uncut stone set in concrete; the stones
may be flat or odd-shaped or even look like potatoes.
One of the problems with rough-surfaced stairs of

this type is that many pockets are created where water collects and can seep in around stones. This will freeze in the winter (in northern areas) and crack the stone or cement, which in turn allows more seepage and so on, until the stair or retaining wall deteriorates and collapses. Check for loose stone and broken or missing pieces; also look for moss or other growth, which would indicate excessive moisture and poor, or no, drainage. Rough stone walls built without mortar do not usually have the same shifting or self-destructing problems; water can run through the spaces in the stones, and whatever freezes can expand without doing too much damage. The freezing merely fills the gaps between stones with ice.

Concrete Stairs

Concrete stairs that have been cast in place should have no openings for water to collect. You should look for cracks or holes and try to determine if the pitch is correct: water should run off the front edges and not back toward the risers. Green stains, growth, or mildew would indicate a spot where water sits. Precast stairs have a very clean, factory-line look that aids in identification. They may come in different styles and may be smooth or have small pebbles showing on the surface. Precast stairs may be found in newer housing and in many instances are used to replace badly broken original stairs, or used where some upgrading or exterior renovations have taken place.

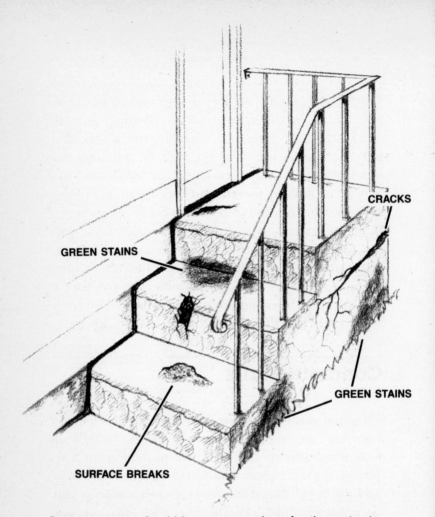

CRACKS

GREEN STAINS

GREEN STAINS

SURFACE BREAKS

Concrete steps should have no openings for the water to collect; look for breaks or other defects.

In addition to the physical condition of the stairs themselves, you should look at the condition of the side supports. Often precast steps are installed with no regard for the holding ability of the sides. If the original steps were lighter in weight, there may be some compression or shifting of the support system.

Limestone Stairs

Limestone stairs and side supports usually develop fewer problems than most, because of the density of the stone and the fact that they are usually in larger sections, with fewer seams or joints. Look for washed-out mortar between risers and treads and between large stone blocks. Long neglect and poor repair policies may be the cause of shifting and water damage to under-supports and possibly leakage into the cellar.

Bluestone or Slate Stairs

Bluestone or slate tends to flake off in small sheets and on flat surfaces, such as stairs and walks. It is important to look for cracks or holes that would allow water to get under the surface and lift it. The flaking is a problem since cement patches rarely hold. If you find large pieces of slate missing, you may have to replace an entire block or section.

Brownstone Stairs

Brownstone steps are usually found with buildings dating from Victorian times up to the 1930s. Brownstone is reddish-brown sandstone and porous and

with age tends to flake away and dissolve. By this
time, most brownstone steps will have patched areas.
Besides looking for patches and loose sections, look
for places that are lifted in small sheets. If the steps
and, for that matter, the brownstone face of a building are tapped with a rigid instrument, you can
discover hollow spots where the stone face is no
longer firmly fastened to under-stone or brickwork.

Hollow-sounding spots are indicators of stone
that will need to be replaced in a short time. Where
there is defective stone, that section and any other
poor surrounding stone will have to be cut back to
solid material and the opened area replaced with
either brownstone-colored cement (matching color
or texture may be a problem) or any color cement
and then the front of the building or the steps must
be painted.

A better, but far more costly, repair is to have
the entire front wall or stair facing removed and
everything refaced in a brownstone-colored cement.
This eliminates the color-matching problem and also
partly ensures that another old section of wall will
not fail where spot patching is done.

At this point, most things concerning external
aspects of buildings have been covered. We are now
ready for an internal examination of the property,
starting at the front door.

II.
The
Interior

Front Door

Normally there is one entry door, or there may be a storm and screen door in front of the actual door. There may be another inner door in a vestibule or foyer. Older brownstones or turn-of-the-century buildings could have one or two sets of double doors ten feet high at the top of a set of stairs leading to a parlor floor. The entrance might be an ornate iron gate under a stoop with one or two sets of doors behind the gate.

Look for the same things, whatever the type of entrance door. The door should operate smoothly and not bind when opened or closed. It shouldn't have to be slammed or pushed to get it to shut and latch.

Now that you are inside the building but still at the doorway, did you notice if there was a door button, and if so, does the bell, buzzer, or chime work?

Where you start inside a building makes little difference: either go up and work down, or go from the basement or cellar and up. Unless the building you are looking at is all on one level with the heating plant, water tank, and other utilities all on the same level, you will have one or more internal flights of stairs.

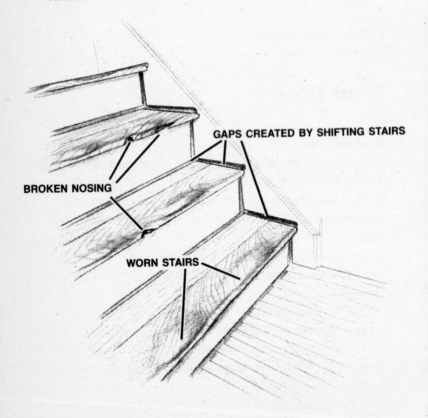

Interior wood stairs may have gaps or spaces which may have been caused by movement in the main supporting beam of the building.

Interior Stairs

Stair treads may be made of any number of types of wood: hardwoods such as oak take the best finishes and wear the longest. Look for worn or broken edges. Look for dish-shaped surfaces if steps are of soft wood. If the stairs are carpeted, it becomes difficult or impossible to determine the condition of the wood. Often stair carpet is a runner that leaves some wood exposed on both sides of the steps, and this may allow you to make a partial visual inspection.

If there is access to the wood stairs, then look for gaps where risers and treads meet. Often stairs are loosened by carpet installers and the points where risers and treads meet are separated because too much pressure has been applied during carpet installation. Moving risers and treads back into their original positions can be a messy and costly job, which will entail the removal or replacement of plaster or plasterboard underneath the steps. This must be removed to allow access to the blocks and wedges that hold stairs in place.

The closed side of the staircase—where treads and risers fit into an angled board—is called a *stringer*. This board is nailed to the wall and is one of the important support elements of any staircase: risers and treads fit into slots or notches and are held in place from underneath. The outside stringer is supported at the top and bottom of the stairwell, and treads and risers fit into open cutouts.

As you walk up or down any staircase you should

be able to see or feel a slope that is out of a level plane. While you are going up or down stairs, carefully note the wall-side stringer to see if risers or treads have pulled out of the slots and to see if there is any movement at the point where the risers or treads fit into the slots. Wedges or metal brackets are installed to reinforce and hold risers and treads in place. These repairs should be looked upon as temporary and not as a permanent cure for shifting or sagging stairs. Stairs that are tilted toward the center of the building, away from the solid wall or out of the stringer, and stairs that have dropped or shifted usually relate to a problem in the main beam or bearing beam running along and underneath the stair wall. This beam would be located in the cellar and is the load-bearing support to the building. It is possible that there is more than one main or bearing beam to a building. A bearing beam or wall normally runs in an opposite direction, or crossways to the floor or ceiling joists. It is usually supported at the ends and at various points along the length. A main beam, where it is visible in a cellar, may be supported by solid steel columns; brick or block piers; and in very old brownstone-type buildings by brick arches. Where the main beam is wood, insect or rot damage to the ends will allow the beam to drop or shift and thus affect the stairs, causing any of the above problems. In addition to permitting stairs to shift, radical movement to the main beam can cause internal walls to move and can be the cause of cracked walls and ceilings.

Stairs in older buildings are supported on hidden beams that are fastened in the openings of the stairwells. These support beams were nailed into the openings and onto bridge beams. Because of the movement in stairs during normal use, the beams that support the stairs slowly shift. Where they were nailed with old "cut" nails, the shift up and down causes the nail, which has fairly sharp, square corners, to enlarge the nail hole and then either the stair moves or the support beam moves and allows the staircase to drop. Support beams can dry out or split, and that can also cause a shift to the stairs. Any badly shifted or tilted staircase can prove to be an expensive repair. Badly shifted stairs that feel solid and appear to be stable can move at any time and may even drop.

Another fairly common cause of shifting is if the side stringer has come away from the wall for some reason, causing the stairs to drop. Look for spaces along the top of the molding or stringer. Spongy or loose stairs are obvious problems and are an indication of some movement by a support member.

Attic

The top of the building directly under the roof may contain an attic or crawl space. Either or both may be reached by a ladder or stairs that may be fixed in place or fold up into a trapdoor. Access may be through a ceiling trap in a closet where no ladder is provided.

Ladders

Permanent ladders should be firmly fastened at the top and bottom with solidly fixed rungs or stairs. Folding stairs covered by a trapdoor or wood panel should be raised and lowered to get some idea of the ease or difficulty of opening the trap. The stairs should be unfolded and folded back to see that they do so without binding. Walking up and down the stairs, you should get some feel of how solid the treads are and if bolts or fastening rods are tight and solid. Folding stairs are made of rather thin material, and many of them are poorly constructed. You should look for cracked or split side rails that may cause stairs to loosen and possibly collapse completely under strain. Both folding or permanent stairs should have sturdy, solid handrails.

An attic crawl space may be just that, and you may find that the only access is visual. One thing to look for in the crawl area is any obvious sign of roof leaks. Using a flashlight, you should be able to see many or all of the roof joists and a large number of roof boards. Victorian-era row houses have, as a rule, very little space between the roof boards and the top-floor ceiling. There may be only a ten- or twelve-inch space, which would allow for very little visual inspection of roof joists or roof boards. One cannot crawl into the area without the danger of going through the top-floor ceiling.

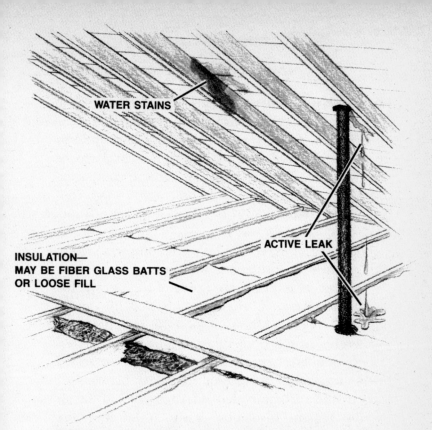

WATER STAINS

ACTIVE LEAK

**INSULATION—
MAY BE FIBER GLASS BATTS
OR LOOSE FILL**

Attics may show water stains in different sections. Leaks may occur around chimneys, plumbing bents or other items that go through the roof.

Roof Insulation

You should look for obviously wet areas and stained or water-streaked beams, joists, and roof boards. Look for wet marks or streaking where chimneys, plumbing vents, ducting, or other items including skylights go through a roof. While checking for leaks, look for insulation. In an unfinished attic or in a roof crawl space, there should be insulation on the "floor" area. Many very old buildings have little or no insulation, and if there is any, it is likely to be mineral wool. Mineral wool can become compacted over time or because it has become wet through roof leaks, thus diminishing its efficiency as insulation. Years ago insulation was also installed because "it was a good thing to have," but little attention was paid to the thickness or insulation "R" factor.

Air spaces in insulation is one of the factors that determine efficiency. Highly compacted fill can be improved by the addition of loose-fill material, such as fiberglass or rolled fiberglass with no vapor barrier.

A complete lack of insulation can be corrected by the installation of loose-fill fiberglass, blankets, or batts of the recommended thickness, or "R" factor for the region. Insulation is also a factor where air-conditioning is concerned and acts as a buffer between the sun and the inside of the building in summer heat, even without air-conditioning.

In an attic area that has a floor and room to stand but is mainly used for storage, try to determine if there is insulation under the floorboards.

In a finished attic, where walls and ceilings have been installed, you should make some attempt to determine if there is any insulation. If there is no access for a visual examination, inquire directly to the sellers. If insulation was installed while they lived in the building, or if they had it done, they may have a bill or other proof. Many finished attic areas have additional storage spaces where the roof pitch is too low to allow standing. These areas are good places to check for insulation and, of course, roof leaks. Attics and crawl spaces should have some ventilation to expel built-up hot air in summer. There should be louvered vents at the front and the rear of attic or crawl areas under roofs. In flat-roofed buildings, skylights with louvered sides or opened hip vents serve the same purpose. A suburban building might have a fan set into the attic window or a louvre set into the wall that opens as the fan goes on. There might be vents set in the soffit (the overhang of a roof in a suburban house) around the building and extending into an attic. You may also find that the attic has one minimal window or no provision for any ventilation at all.

Old Wiring

In older buildings, built prior to the 1930s, you may find very old and obsolete wiring in the attic area; it is called knob-and-tube and is easy to identify since it is made of two fairly heavy single strands of wire supported on porcelain insulators. These are set several feet apart, and the wires run parallel, six inches apart. Restrictions on the continued use of this type of wiring will vary with local building or electrical codes. One problem with this type of wiring is that insulation tends to be very dry and brittle: it can and does fall off. Another problem is the possibility of one or both wires being broken or damaged if any renovation or construction work is done in the immediate area.

The wire is a potential shock or fire hazard if one strand breaks or if the insulation is abraded or missing. You can find sections of this old and close-to-original wiring still extant in the attics of buildings even where the electrical system has been upgraded to some degree.

If you find knob-and-tube wiring in an attic, try to trace it back and determine if it is still connected and is still in use. It may only have been left in place and may not be connected.

While looking through the attic or crawl space where roof beams or joists are exposed, you should look around for separated joints, sagging or shifted wood members, and for split or cracked elements. The level below the attic in most buildings is a floor with bedrooms and usually one or more bathrooms. Some buildings have a complete apartment on this (or any other) level where zoning is more than one-family, and so there may also be a kitchen.

Walls

Walls or ceilings should be checked for cracking and/or sagging. Ceilings to rooms that are under kitchens or bathrooms should be carefully checked for leak stains or discolored surfaces and for anything that would indicate a leak.

Stained or discolored ceiling areas around heat

risers or in the area of radiators might indicate a leak in the valves or connections of a steam or hot-water radiator.

Efflorescence, the appearance of a powdery substance on a wall or ceiling, is an indicator of leaking from a source on the other side of the wall or ceiling area: water is leaching mineral salts through the surface of finished plaster or cement. It is common to see it on a ceiling in a bathroom where there is a leak in the bathroom above.

Floors

Flooring type and condition should be checked on this and other levels. Carpeted, tiled, and linoleum-covered floors will make it difficult or impossible to determine wood type and condition. Asking the owner may not give you an accurate answer.

Linoleum or resilient tiles can be cemented directly over an original wood floor. Removing these to have the floor finished can be a mess and in some cases may damage the wood surface. Usually resilient tiles are cemented over Masonite or plywood that is nailed to the wood flooring. Removal is easier than with tile cemented directly on to the floor, since the Masonite or plywood comes up in large pieces and there is not any mastic on the original floor. There will just be some nail holes where the plywood was fastened. If you have no desire for exposed wood floors, carpeting may be placed over tile.

Floors can be oak, pine, maple, or nearly any type of wood, or any combination of woods. A floor can be plain plywood that was always meant to be carpeted, or it can be resilient tile over plywood, which was an original installation and always intended for tiles. A lower-level floor can be simply a cement slab covered with carpet or tile.

Ceilings

Ceilings may be covered with many different types of material. Acoustical tiles may be stapled to furring strips or can be installed in metal channels hung from the original ceiling. A ceiling may be pressed steel (often referred to as tin) with a design embossed on it. Sometimes ceilings are covered by plastic panels or other panels installed in grids. A ceiling may be wood planks or plywood squares and, of course, more commonly, plasterboard (Sheetrock) or plaster.

Walls may also be plaster over wood or wire lath. They may be plasterboard or covered with wood paneling. There may be wallpaper, fabric, or plastic-coated fabrics or paper, and again, they can be covered with other types or combinations of material.

Regardless of the surface coverings, you should be looking for leak marks or stains. Look for discoloration or streaks and rust marks: be aware of any color other than the color of the material itself. Odd colors on a surface are indicators of leaks, either active, or old ones that have been repaired.

The most common wall or ceiling surface you will encounter is plasterboard, also called Sheetrock, gypsum board, or just wallboard. In this type of covering, long visible seams or tape joints that show are indicators of poor installation or poor finishing. Nail heads that show or "dimples" where nails have been installed might indicate a poorly installed panel or one that has moved or shifted. If you find a line of nails that have "popped" or show partly through the covering joint compound, there is a very good chance that the beam or joist holding the plasterboard has twisted or shifted for some reason. Sagged or bulged plasterboard may have been installed on insufficient support members or may not have enough nails to hold it in place, or possibly has become wet from above and dropped from the weight of saturation.

Cracks in corners of walls and ceilings where the crack has gone through the paper tape that closes the joints or seams in plasterboard might be an indication of a serious shifting problem somewhere in the building.

Unless there has been impact damage to plasterboard, leaving a hole, most cracking will be along a joint or seam, or in a corner where walls join, or where walls and ceilings meet. Thin hairline cracks are probably in the paint surface. Plaster walls and ceilings predate plasterboard and are usually found in older buildings, or in buildings that may have been custom-built.

Plaster in older buildings was installed over thin wood strips (laths) that were nailed to studding or joists. Old plaster was usually put up in three layers.

The first coat over the lath was a rough coat and of a porous type, with a texture like sand—in the oldest installations this coat was fibered with hair or some other mineral fiber. The second coat was about the same texture as the first but without fiber content. The surface of this coat was scratched or scarred to give it a very rough texture, so that the last, or polished, finish coat would adhere tightly. The build-up of plaster coats made some older wall and ceiling surfaces ⅝″ to 1″ thick and thus very heavy. The weight of plaster can cause large cracks to develop if there is any separation of plaster from the lath or movement of laths on the supporting studding.

Cracks can and do move slightly or shrink, and as a building expands or contracts with weather changes, so do the inside walls and ceilings. Age is also a factor to some degree, and also the slight absorption of airborne moisture. Cracks or loosening can develop because of impact to the surface, or even because of heavy hammering to adjacent areas. Shifting of any support member in the building, leaks, or the normal deterioration due to age can cause cracking and subsequent sagging to occur.

Look carefully for sagging plaster and for long or deep cracks, either one of which could mean that the plaster wall or ceiling will need replacement or extensive patching.

Missing or peeling surface layers of plaster over what appears to be a sound background may be caused by a finishing coat of plaster coming away from the base plaster. This usually happens where a thin coating of plaster has been applied over an old plaster surface to resurface poor or cracking walls or ceilings. This can be avoided if the plasterer uses a bonding agent. If you have to redo an area, you should make sure it is correctly applied. Again, you should be aware that you may have to redo such a peeling surface. In the case of badly cracked or sagging surfaces, you may have to totally redo an area. Wire lath as a support for plaster came into use well after wood lath strips. Unlike wood lath, which was supplied in relatively short and narrow pieces and installed with spaces between the strips, wire lath comes in eight-foot lengths two feet wide.

You cannot tell visually if there is a metal lath base to a plastered area. You might find metal lath and plaster in buildings built prior to the early fifties or in more expensive, custom housing. One advantage to the wire lath used for plastering is the length of material and its greater coverage of supporting joists or studding. Because the metal does not expand or twist as wood lath can, the chances of cracking are reduced. There is also less likelihood of sagging or separated plaster. Short of cutting a hole in a wall or ceiling, you will probably not be able to tell what the plaster has been installed over. There is another installation used frequently, and that is gypsum board, nailed over studding and then plastered. The board came in four-foot lengths and had factory-stamped holes throughout it, which served the same purpose as the spaces between laths to hold plaster in place. You will not be able to tell without making a hole through the surface. Because any plaster wall, regardless of content or material, cost much more to install and finish than plasterboard, you will probably not find it in buildings erected after the early fifties or in row or development housing. Costs of labor and material and the relative ease of installation have made plasterboard the most commonly used interior finishing material.

Because of the longer lengths and widths plasterboard comes in, and its greater spanning ability, cracks through the surface are less frequent. Cracks that do appear would normally occur where boards join, if the installation or finishing was faulty. Problems with plasterboard occur when nail heads or seams show. This indicates incorrect nailing (too few nails used) or that the studding was not rigid. Unless there has been a major structural shift or other structural problem in the building, renailing will usually correct most of these problems. If you are serious about buying a building with plasterboard walls or ceilings with any of these problems, you probably should have the seller correct them and then go back to inspect the finished work.

On rare occasions you may come across a wood-paneled ceiling or a room with very old fitted paneling and intricate moldings to match.

Heating

In an area that requires winter heating, you should check whether there is a permanent heating unit. Regardless of the type of heating, you should turn it on to be sure that it works. If you are looking at a building in the winter, it will probably be on. You should then check to see that the individual radiators, baseboard units, heating ducts, or whatever, are working.

Buildings that use electric heat usually have individual thermostats or switches in each room, and the heat can be supplied by baseboard units, glass panels, heaters with fans, or radiant heating panels. A central heating unit will, of course, send heat throughout the building. If there is a separately zoned heating area, it may be turned down at the individual thermostat. There may be times in the summer when the air temperature is so high that the thermostat will not respond and the heat will not go on. On these hot days it might not be a bad idea to contact whoever maintains or services the unit to get their opinion of its condition.

While checking the heat in the individual rooms, look for plug-in, auxiliary heating devices, which might indicate inadequate heat from the main heating source or a very cold or drafty area. You should determine that each room has some source of heat, even if you feel that you will never turn it on. In a very severe winter you may wish that you had some way to heat a cold room.

It is very easy to overlook a heat source when looking at a room full of someone else's furniture. In very old, urban housing, town houses or brownstones, where forced air heating is used, it is not uncommon to find that there is no heating in front or rear hall rooms. Over a period of time renovations and alterations to these buildings turned these areas into kitchens or bathrooms, and often no provision was made to extend the warm-air ducting or to provide another heat source. Many renovations were done where a built-in electric heater was provided, but there are an equal number where this was not done, especially in cases where a renovation was done for rental or speculation and where the owner or renovator never lived in the building.

Bathroom Heat

A bathroom can be very cold at two A.M. in winter, so check carefully. A seller may be using a portable electric heater that is kept in a closet when not in use.

While checking radiators, look for rust streaks around valves (both shut-off and air valves). Rusting on any radiator surface could indicate a crack or hole in one of the sections. Look at the floor areas around radiators. They may give some indication of a leak, which could show up as a dark section of wood.

A radiator that has been leaking for a long period of time can also cause damage or deterioration to wood flooring. A section of finished floor can be rotted, or there might be rot damage to subflooring or a floor joist. A spongy floor under a carpet around a radiator would be a possible indication of such damage.

Cold radiators or radiators that are only partially heated should be looked upon with suspicion if others in the area are totally hot. Radiators in a steam system may have to be repitched, and those in a hot-water system might have to be bled or purged of air. A circulating, or forced air, system does not have radiators; instead there are heating ducts throughout the building that terminate in louvres—usually in the walls of individual rooms. Louvres can be in ceilings or in the floor. Rooms in a building with a hot-air system without grilles or louvres will have no heat. Because grilles usually are set in walls and are often behind furniture, they can easily be overlooked or not looked for at all—the assumption being that buildings that require heat in winter will have heat in all areas.

Heat Vents

There are many very old hot-air systems still in use in older buildings, and many of these do not have a fan to move and circulate the heated air. The oldest units (some may be original installations) depended upon reverse gravity, or the fact that warm air rises, to heat the building without the aid of any additional push. This type of system may make an area around an outlet grille comfortable or even relatively warm, while the far side of the room can be much cooler or even cold. The ceiling and a few feet below it may be very warm, while the lower part of the room, where you would like warm feet, can be cold or uncomfortable. At the midpoint, warm and cold air do not merge, and the heat just hangs.

New or upgraded older systems will have a fan to force heated air through the ducts, and you will be able to feel the heat coming out of the grille with some force. Circulating hot-air systems require return grilles or louvres to allow cooler air, which the warm air forces down, to get back to the heating plant so that it can be heated and circulate again as warmed air. Many older systems have no such returns and merely heat air that floats down.

Return grilles are located on the lowest level of a building above the cellar and may be set into the floor. Returns must be free and unobstructed. If you cannot see it, ask for its location. If the heating system has been upgraded from an older unit, it is possible that a grille was never installed—unlikely but not impossible. Occasionally a floor return will be covered with a rug. The owner may not be aware that it is a return duct and thinks it is for heat: he decided he would not need heat in the small spare room and would rather have the carpet without a hole cut in it. In a small building there may be one central grille to heat the entire building.

The same ducting and grille system may be used for a central air-conditioning system. This is possible when it has been installed as an addition at a later date, or if it was part of the original building.

Ducting in walls and ceilings, along with louvres or grilles, may be part of the central air-conditioning system, despite the type of heating the building uses.

In such instances it can be assumed that the air-conditioning was added after the heating unit was installed.

Electric heating usually has a thermostat or switch to shut down or turn up heat to individual rooms.

Steam, or circulating hot-water systems, will have valves to each individual unit (in very low baseboard units that are sometimes impossible to reach or turn).

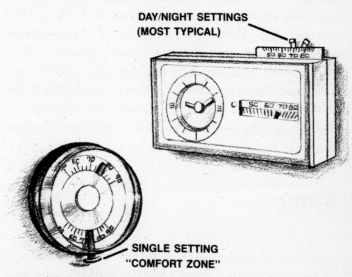

DAY/NIGHT SETTINGS (MOST TYPICAL)

SINGLE SETTING "COMFORT ZONE"

Heating thermoststs may have a one setting "comfort zone" or more elaborate multiple settings.

Thermostats

If there is a central air-conditioning system in the building, it should be turned on and tried. If it is part of a hot-air heating system, this may not be possible in winter when the heat is on. Somewhere in the building there will be a thermostat to control the heating or cooling. A heating thermostat may be a simple, small, round unit with a minimum of settings or numbers and only one setting for days or nights, called and marked "comfort zone." The thermostat may be of the very newest transistorized style, with multiple settings that can be varied for different needs or situations. Whatever the type or style of unit, you should be most concerned with its age and whether it is working. There are still thermostats being used that appear to date back to the invention of electricity: the clocks do not work, the contacts are dirty, and they run very erratically, which affects the heating and also the heating unit. You may need to buy the house a new thermostat as a housewarming gift.

Wiring

A difficult thing to find in a room full of furniture is an electrical outlet. Ideally there should be one outlet three feet away from where you want it on any wall. In the real world very old buildings may have one to a room, and some rooms may have none at all. Rooms may have a maze of extension cords running along baseboards from one outlet, and that one outlet may be powering half a dozen more outlets in a room. In very old, neglected urban housing, where little if anything has ever been done to upgrade the building, many extension cords may be powered by a ceiling fixture: cords draped down from the ceiling to a tabletop for a radio and along the ceiling and wall for a hot plate or lamp. Any of these situations probably mean extensive rewiring or at least the removal of the extension cords as potential fire hazards.

Many of the ceiling electrical boxes in the older urban buildings will, in addition to wire, have a gas pipe connected to the house gas system. Often gas is still in the pipe. Before any electrical work is done a plumber should be consulted. Where the building originally had gaslights, the gas lines were left and lighting was, in many cases, by both gas and electric. Gas had been around for a long time, and electricity, being very new, might not last, so both options were left open.

Renovations to older buildings (those around the turn of the century) often uncover gas lines inside walls that supplied gas to chandeliers and wall sconces. If you are looking at a Victorian-era building, you may come across a gas "arm" in a cellar or other part of the building. It is not a good idea to turn the gas key control to see if it works; often the metal is very brittle or partly rusted and the key will break off and you may be standing in a fairly strong stream of gas with no way to shut it off, short of turning off the main gas flow to the building.

Electrical work done in newer buildings, or upgraded electrical work, would normally follow the guidelines of a local building code, and that would provide for enough outlets to conform to code speci-

110 VOLTS—UNGROUNDED

110/220 VOLTS—GROUNDED
THREE–PRONG—30 AMPS

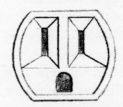

110 VOLTS—GROUNDED
THREE–PRONG

110/220 VOLTS—GROUNDED
THREE–PRONG—50 AMPS

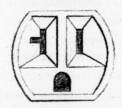

110 VOLTS—GROUNDED
THREE–PRONG—20 AMPS

220 VOLTS—GROUNDED
THREE-PRONG—30 AMPS

110 VOLTS—UNGROUNDED—VERY
EARLY OUTLET BEFORE
PRONGS WERE STANDARDIZED

All outlets fall into one of the categories pictured.

fications. Electrical work should have been done by a
licensed electrical contractor who would follow the
national or local code, whichever had precedence.
One or the other of these will usually detail the
number of outlets for a wall or room and also
probably the current-carrying capacity.

New or newer electrical outlets have, in addition
to a pair of parallel slots, a round opening for the
ground lug on appliance or other plugs. These three
prong outlets are often mistaken for, or referred to,
as 220-volt outlets.

220-volt outlet slots are not parallel or straight
in line with each other: the flat slots are set at an
angle so that a normal plug will not fit. Plugging in
the average appliance that requires 110 volts to operate it will probably destroy the appliance in a fire-
works display of sparks and noise.

Normally appliances, portable power tools, hair
dryers, etc., use 110 volts. A very large window air
conditioner, an electric stove, or a large electric clothes
dryer probably would require a 220-volt outlet. Visible outlets that are larger than usual and have angled slots are probably 220-volt for heavy-use items.
If you are not sure about an outlet, ask the broker or
seller. If you are not satisfied with the answer, you
should hold out for a better answer. If a regular plug
(a lamp, for example) does not fit the outlet because
of the prong or slot shape, then it is probably for a
220-volt appliance.

Buildings that date prior to the late 1930s may
still have some old or original outlets with two sets of
slots—one overlapping the other. One pair of slots

will be parallel and one pair will be in line with each other, looking like a long, divided single slot. The parallel pair will fit the usual two-prong plug. The two shaped outlets were put in before plugs became standardized. It is possible that the outlets can be replaced with new ones with ground lugs. In a very old building where the old wiring has been retained or not totally replaced, you may find single porcelain outlets. These can usually be replaced with grounded outlets, since the metal connector box is a standard size and a new outlet and cover should fit. One problem that might be encountered in replacing older outlets is that the wire insulation tends to become brittle with age, and it is also possible that a wire will snap. Again, any electrical work should be done by a licensed electrician.

Pull Chains

As you are walking through the building make note of any pull-chain-operated ceiling lights. You may want to replace these with wall switches. You should also be looking for and checking wall switches. They should be convenient to doors or openings and, ideally, be under your hand at the spot you automatically reach for. Shortage of outlets or wall switches and any necessary upgrading of the electrical system will be fairly expensive and messy: cable has to go around or through studding or joists, and this requires cutting holes to pull cable to its destination.

Holes have to be opened for outlet and switch boxes, and after all the work is completed, all the openings will have to be plastered shut.

If the floor you are on is a self-contained living unit or a totally separate apartment from the rest of the building, then there should also be a circuit breaker or fuse box to control the power, situated where permissible by local code. Electrical control boxes should not be in bathrooms or other wet areas and should not be hidden in closets or cabinets where the fuses or breaker switches are not easily accessible.

In a building that houses more than one family, the breaker or fuse box is often located in the cellar, and often this is not open to the occupants of the building (other than the owner). As an owner-occupant, you may be called at any time of the day or night to replace a fuse or switch a breaker back on. The cost of moving a circuit breaker box up from the cellar can be fairly high and will, of course, entail some damage to walls or ceilings. If you are going to do any renovation or alteration to the building soon after purchase, that would be the best time to move the box(es) up to the apartment(s).

Bathrooms

In recent years bathrooms have gone beyond the merely functional and in many instances have become decorators' playing fields. You might find, in addition to the usual toilet, washbasin, and tub, a bidet, a wet and dry steam unit, a sauna or hot tub—or even a whirlpool bath. There may be a large stall shower with a dozen shower heads coming at you from all directions.

Water Pressure

Whatever you find in a bathroom should be in working order. Where possible, everything should be turned on and tried. Water should be turned on at the basin and tub to see what the water pressure is like; if it is poor and drops off when the toilet is flushed and starts to refill, or if it drops off when another water faucet is turned on in the building, you may have an expensive plumbing alteration to contend with. A drastic drop in water pressure, or generally poor pressure, might indicate a water main that needs replacement or the need for new plumbing risers inside the building.

Water Drainage

Running water in the basin, tub, or shower while flushing the toilet will give you some indication of how rapidly fixtures drain. Slow or sluggish drainage, or water that backs up in the tub or shower, would indicate some blockage in the drain lines going to the main sewer line (stack) and probably some blocked elbows from one or more of the fixtures.

A drainage problem in a lower floor directly over a cellar, or in a single-level dwelling, might indicate a blocked main sewer line that would have to be snaked out to the street sewer.

Sluggish or slow draining in a building that drains into a septic tank (rather than to a sewer system) would be an indication that there is some problem either in the waste pipe that goes to the tank or in the septic tank itself. The system may need to be cleaned or need other servicing: it is not impossible that the septic tank needs to be rebuilt. Any major septic system repairs will be very expensive. If you have any doubts or questions regarding proper functioning, you should seek the advice of a local repair or maintenance service that specializes in such tank work.

Plumbing Vents

While checking to see how well a drain to a tub, sink, or basin works, you should allow water to be held in the fixture by means of the drain plug or whatever the fixture depends on, and then drain it away in volume, rather than just letting the faucet run: noisy, bubbling, gurgling drainage would indicate a blocked vent or, more likely, no vent at all.

Plumbing sewer lines should be air-vented through the roof of a building to fresh air. You can usually

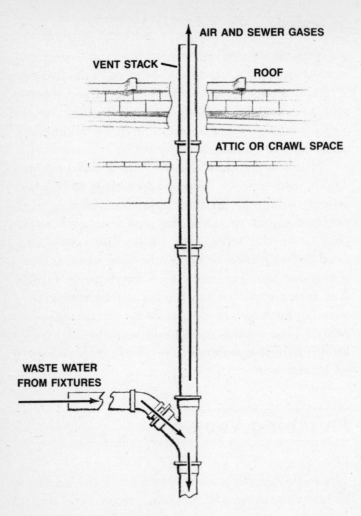

Typical sewer/vent system.

see the vent pipe going through an attic or crawl space and through the roof. On the outside of the building or on the roof itself, it will be visible: a pipe usually about four inches in diameter, but it may be as small as one inch. The presence of a vent pipe does not always indicate it is connected, especially in a building that has been renovated over and over. Draining a fixture is one of the best indicators because of the noise produced in a nonvented situation.

Unvented waste lines can cause noisy or slow drainage, can cause a tub or basin to back up to some degree, and can cause a methane gas odor from drain openings. Because methane burns and can explode, there is a very slim possibility that under the right conditions it might do so in a kitchen or bathroom.

Venting a plumbing waste line and venting a room are two separate and distinct items. Kitchens and bathrooms that have a window, even if it opens onto an air shaft, are no problem since (unless the window has been sealed) it can be opened to allow for an exchange of air.

An inside bathroom or kitchen that has no window will need some way to manage air exchange. This is done by a mechanical fan connected to a system of ducting that finds its way to a fresh air source, either through the roof or through an exterior wall.

If there is a fan and duct system in a bathroom, it should be arranged so that the fan goes on when the light is turned on. A bathroom or kitchen could be vented by a nonmechanical means where a duct depends on warm air rising into it. These types will usually, but not always, have a rotating roof fan that is wind-driven to help move the air up and out. There can be an electrically operated fan in a roof enclosure to move air by drawing it up, rather than a fan in a room that pushes it out. Any mechanical fan should remove more moist air than one that only depends on gravity.

Regardless of the method used, there must be some way to air-vent a bathroom; without some way to remove moisture-laden air you will develop a mildew problem, which, in addition to staining walls or wallpaper, smells musty and looks terrible. Moisture in a bathroom will cause things to rust and woodwork to rot. The warm, wet environment is an ideal insect breeding ground.

Heat Source

As a reminder from a previous section: older urban-house bathrooms (especially in row houses) have probably been added and are not original. Many of these bathrooms are in areas of the building that never had heat—such as the center portion of a floor or a front or rear hall. You should check and make sure that there is some heat source—if you are lucky, it will have a radiator or a louvre. There may be no more than a steam or hot-water riser. If there is no heat, you may have to add an electric heater, one that is built into the wall or the ceiling. If this heater is needed, you will probably have to bring in an electrical line from the nearest fuse or circuit breaker box and, again, you should be aware of the cost, plus the cost of repairing the holes where cable has been drawn through the wall and/or ceiling.

Tiles

The most substantial and longest-wearing floor and wall surface for a bathroom is ceramic tile. If there is a tiled floor, look for cracks, low sections, or broken, missing, or badly patched areas. If there is carpeting on the floor, by all means look under it. Cracks in an old ceramic-tile floor usually occurred soon after installation. These were probably caused because joists were cut to install plumbing or due to the weight of cement used for tile installation. The weight of the tile, cement, and a cast-iron tub may have bowed or cracked one or more floor joists. If the floor feels soft or appears to move to any degree, there is probably another, more serious, problem. Check wall tiles for loose or uneven tiles. Look for poorly replaced or patched areas, which would be an indication of some problem in the support members of the wall. It could also be a problem caused by leaks behind the tile surface. Carefully check the grout joints, especially in an area you have a question about. Missing grout, or a gap between the top of the tub and wall, can cause leakage problems to walls and ceilings below. Pushing against or gently tapping a tile wall, especially around tub faucets or spouts, may give you some clue to loose or poorly fastened tiles. A hollow sound might be an indicator that tile has lost its bond with the underlying wall or that the wall itself may have some rot or other deterioration problem. Only removal of suspect tiles can allow inspection of the supporting wall under the tile to determine the cause of any suspected problem. Tub or stall shower wall tiles can be in such poor condition that by pressing against them, wall tiles will move and may even fall. Wall tiles installed from the late fifties and later may not be installed on a concrete base but with a waterproof mastic over plasterboard or possibly plywood.

One of the problems with these installations is that moisture-resistant plasterboard and/or exterior plywood with waterproof glue was not always used—especially since the mastic made the installation of tiles on some type of backing board an attractive, do-it-yourself project. Unfortunately, while many do-it-yourselfers may be good workers, they are not always aware of the correct materials needed or available for specific jobs. Unless the bathroom you are looking at is fairly new and the owner tells you proudly that he did it, you will not be able to tell what materials were used. Once any type of plasterboard is painted or tiled, you cannot tell if it is a moisture-resistant board or not, without cutting a hole in it and seeing the inner core. You need to be familiar with what the inside of plasterboard looks like.

If regular plasterboard was used, the lower tiles and the lower section of the wall over the tub edge are liable to be soft or may show a mildew stain and will have a musty smell. Any soft or "moving" tiled bathroom walls should be suspect, and you should be aware of the fact that you may have to replace the tile and the backing behind the tile.

Another, newer type of backing board for tile, called "wonder board," is a composition of fiberglass and cement: tiles are installed over this board using a thin-set cement or waterproof mastic. Because the fiberglass should be moisture-proof and the board fairly thick and rigid, there should be no problem of deteriorated walls if the studding and installation were done correctly.

Bathroom walls may be of many other materials besides ceramic tile. There are plastic tiles which are glued up; or there may be a large Masonite panel with squares embossed into the surface that has been enameled and looks rather like tile from a distance or until you tap it. If either of these has been correctly installed and sealed, they should give reasonable service but will not last nearly as long as a ceramic wall. Plastic tiles tend to pop off a wall a few at a time: either the cement ages poorly or they expand too much under heat and then contract rapidly when the temperature drops.

Tile Board

Tile board is easily worn away when cleaned with scouring cleansers and will deteriorate badly if an edge is often very wet.

Formica Walls

At one time Formica wall coverings were used, with matching trim moldings at seams and tub or wall edges. If these were correctly installed and sealed, they can last fairly well. Again, they may become discolored or badly worn if scouring powders abrade the surface.

On all of the above coverings look carefully for visible mildew along edges and for leak stains on ceilings below. Any wall, especially in a wet area like a bathroom, should be checked for potential leakage problems to the areas under them. Bathroom walls may be sealed or varnished wood; they may be marble, slate, or plastic—any material that comes to mind that can be installed and made fairly leak- or water-resistant is liable to be used as a wall covering.

Besides ceramic tile, a bathroom floor may be made of any material that can be made moisture-resistant and hopefully leak-proof. Unfortunately this is not always the case: there could be wood floors with warping and rot problems; linoleum that is loosely fitted; or resilient tiles cemented directly over wood flooring with cracks through the top of the tile.

Bathroom Floors

As with everything else in the building, pay careful attention to the floor: its material and condition. Look for mildew or mold and sniff around for musty or damp smells. Again, look at the condition of ceilings underneath any suspect floor.

Normally the first impression of a bathroom will

be its size and color—somehow general condition, and especially the condition of the fixtures, does not get all the attention it should. Is there a vanity or a basin? If a basin exists, does it have legs or is it a wall-hung unit? If there is a vanity, try the door(s) and drawer(s). The moisture present can warp or swell them to some degree. A wall-hung basin should have a solid feel and not be loose or wobbly. If it is tilted, or if there is a gap between the rear of the basin and the wall, try lifting it gently. If it moves, let it settle back to where it was—you will probably have to have it reset.

Washbasins

Feel under the front lower edge. If there are holes, this basin may have been designed to have legs. If the basin has legs, they should be solid and the basin should not move. Look for stained, worn, or pitted surfaces on the basin and tub. If the building is an old urban building that is, or was, a furnished rooming house, make sure it has a basin in the bathroom.

Toilets

Toilets come in various styles and types. If there is a flushometer (a type where no tank is used), make sure that the water pressure is sufficiently strong to allow the toilet to flush correctly and totally. To test this, drop a loosely rolled wad of toilet paper into the bowl and flush it: a toilet should not need to be flushed more than once to run the paper down. If the water pressure to a flushometer is correct and the paper does not run through, there may be a blocked drain. A blocked drain may be the problem in any toilet that does not flush paper away on the first try.

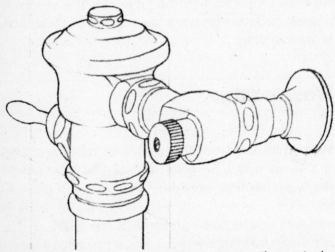

A flushometer requires more water pressure than a tank toilet.

More than likely the toilet will have a tank. This may be the type with a high tank, or it may have a low, sleek profile that is very silent as it flushes and fills. In any tank unit the flush control should work smoothly and the tank should refill fairly rapidly. There should be no dripping or running sound after the tank has refilled. There are some older units where the tank is mounted on the wall above the lower bowl part of the unit. The tank is connected to the bowl by a slightly curved pipe. This pipe and connections between the bowl and pipe, and tank and pipe, should be checked carefully for leaks or seepage. There is still the high tank toilet, where a water box hangs six or eight feet above the toilet itself and is connected with a long pipe that is exposed on the wall. Check for leaking at all pipe connections and for dripping or leaking around the wood tank box. Unless you are committed to this type of unit and love it with all your heart, you should probably anticipate replacing it as a first move. Should you plan to upgrade the bathroom, then you may want to keep it until everything is changed and hope it does not leak.

The material that the fixtures are made of should have some relevance: fiberglass or imitation marble may be easily scratched or the surface quickly dulled by the use of abrasive cleansers. You can usually tell by either the feel, or by visual observation, when a unit is plastic.

Porcelain on steel is probably more common than plastic. While the surface is harder, it can chip if a hard, rigid object, such as a glass bottle, is dropped on it.

If you have any doubts, a magnet will tell you the difference between porcelain and a fiberglass unit. Using an abrasive cleanser will wear the surface away on either kind. The best and longest lasting plumbing fixtures are porcelain on cast iron. Cast iron is the heaviest of all the materials used, and while it may chip if something is dropped on it, the item probably would have to be as heavy as a hammer. A magnet will identify cast iron, as will its solid feel and weight. If a tub is lightly tapped with the foot, it gives a solid thud rather than a hollow, tinny sound, as would a steel-and-porcelain unit. In a very old building, from the country estate to the Victorian-era town house, you might find such exotica as four-inch-thick solid-wall porcelain china, or zinc- or copper-lined tubs and basins surrounded by oak or maple. These are museum pieces at this point in time and have mostly disappeared. In the bathroom, look for an electrical outlet: you may find one in the light fixture, but this may prove to be too high to be convenient. You should test any outlet in a fixture to make sure it works. Bathrooms and other wet areas

Ground Fault Current Interrupters are designed for use in wet areas. They should be in bathrooms, laundry rooms, and exterior outlets.

should have safety outlets, called "ground fault current interrupters." They are outlets with built-in circuit breakers.

While checking water pressure, pay attention to the condition and operation of the faucets. They should turn on and off easily without binding. If faucets are very hard to turn and must be forced to shut them off, they may have been installed incorrectly or the washers may have been replaced with the wrong size. Dripping faucets will need washers or other parts, such as new cartridges in washerless units. Water leaking around faucets, or the housings, may require replacement of the entire faucet unit itself. There are many cheaply made units of thin metal that simply wear out in a short time.

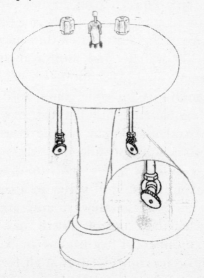

All sinks and toilets should have shut off valves to facilitate repairs.

Faucets and Shutoff Valves

While all of us are familiar with the faucets that control water at its outlet—tub, shower, basin, or sink—and we all know these controls may be turned, pushed, pulled, or tilted to make them operate, there are many people who are not aware of a set of valves that control water to the faucets. Control valves may be located under a sink or basin, or they may be in a closet or cabinet that may not be in the bathroom (or kitchen), or the valves might be behind a wall panel in the hall. The control valve to a toilet normally will be underneath in the feed pipe that supplies water. Never having to make repairs necessitating use of the shutoff valves is a reason for not being aware of them. But often they have never been installed. Renovations and improvements are often done without filing plans and never get inspected by the local authority for code compliance.

Fixtures without shutoff valves may not comply with local codes and may not be considered legal installations in some jurisdictions. Absence of shutoff valves may indicate a less than top-grade plumber. When looking for shutoff valves in a cellar, you are liable to discover that few, if any, are marked to indicate what they control. There may be less than the total number of bathrooms or kitchens, and there may be no control valves at all for a particular bathroom or other area. If there is no valve in a plumbing line to anything that might need repair, the entire house would have to be shut down by turning the main valve off. This would include any repair, even the replacement of a simple washer.

Windows

Windows, for some reason, tend to be ignored or passed over lightly by many people. Even professionals who inspect buildings often ignore them or only give them a superficial glance. While you were checking the outside of the building, you paid some attention to the type and condition of windows. You looked for cracked or missing glass and other window elements. Now that you are inside the building, you should be looking for these items, plus some others.

Attic Windows

An attic window, for example, might be no more than a frame hinged at the top or sides and fastened with a simple hook, or it could be the same type as all the other units in the building. If there is a permanent attic fan, there may not be a window at all but rather a louvre that opens when the fan goes on. Whatever there is should be tried: if it is a window, open and close it. Try the latch and check to see if it has a screen. An attic window might be left open a good part of the summer, and even if the attic is only used for storage, you will not want resident animals or insects.

Attic Fans

If there is an attic fan that operates a louvered window, the fan should be turned on so that you can make sure the louvre opens. Large fans that are used to cool the entire building will need checking to see that the floor, or internal wall, louvre works. Turning on the fan will, of course, let you know if it is in working order, and you will also get an idea of how noisy it will be—is there excessive vibration or other noise that may disturb you? Large attic fans usually have a motor that is separate from the fan blades, and the fan blade unit is driven from a belt system coming off the motor shaft. Before the fan goes on or after it stops, visually check the belt(s) for wear and the possible need for replacement. The fan might be operated by a switch or thermostat, or both.

Where the thermostat is first activated by a switch, check to make sure it works.

The louvres that are part of the attic fan system open when the fan is on and close when it shuts down. They should work very smoothly with no binding and without jerky motion. A properly sized attic fan can be very effective in cooling down and making a building more comfortable in summer.

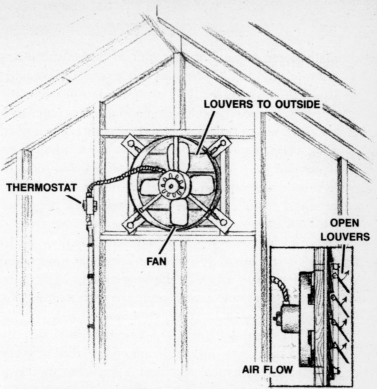

THERMOSTAT

LOUVERS TO OUTSIDE

OPEN LOUVERS

FAN

AIR FLOW

Attic fans may be different sizes and types. Some cool the entire building while other remove only the hot air in the attic.

Windows come in different types, and in turn, the different types come in varying qualities, styles, and finishes. The immediate concern is the condition of the windows and whether or not they work.

Double-hung Windows

The most common type of sliding window is the original double-hung style and the aluminum storm unit. Exterior aluminum storm windows did not normally come as part of the original building but are later additions. The quality and type of available storm units vary greatly. A triple-track unit allows for sashes to be raised and lowered and usually comes with a screen, which remains behind a top or bottom sash. The screen can remain in its own track when both storm sashes are closed. Less expensive units might not have screens, or one glass might have to be removed from the frame when the screen is put in. This, of course, means that the screens have to be removed and stored when both storm sashes are in place. Most storm windows and screens have some type of latch or catch at the lower edge. Make sure that they operate freely and are not jammed or corroded shut, or broken or missing.

Very tight latches can sometimes be freed by using a silicon spray lubricant. Very old or very inexpensive units may not have a latch but merely a small, thin handle to be lifted, and the sashes are held at various heights by friction, rather than by small finger pieces that fit in holes in the frame.

Storm Sashes

A storm sash of reasonable quality, correctly installed, should move freely and not tilt or bind in the tracks. Glass or plastic panels should be intact, and screens should not have holes or tears. Badly pitted aluminum rails or other parts will tend to jam when moved up or down and probably will need cleaning and lubricating. It may seem to take forever, but you should check all the storm windows, as well as the basic house windows. While you have everything open, look outside and check the condition of the caulking where the window frames meet the openings in the building wall. Caulking should be intact—missing sections will allow water to seep in between window framing and the building. Exterior wood windowsills should be checked for any obvious rot or other decay. There can be a condensation problem between storm and regular windows, and the moisture could affect the wood sill or other wood members between both sets of sashes—often the outsides of windows are barely painted or ignored when a building is painted because it means removing the storm sashes. While most of the above is probably more relevant to an older building, or where there are two sets of sashes, points such as fit, operating condition, and caulking would still apply to any windows.

Double-hung windows slide up and down in a pair of wood tracks and are kept separated by a wood "parting" strip. They usually have a center catch where the two halves meet. In the very oldest original installations the upper and lower sashes slide in the wood frames or tracks and have to be held to prevent one section from crashing to the bottom. The center catch prevents them from dropping when the window is closed. A small wood wedge has to be put in place to open them partway. You may still find windows like this in an attic or in an outbuilding away from the main building. There are also buildings owned by purists who will not change anything that is visible.

There are very new, wood, wood-and-vinyl, or metal double-hung sashes that have insulated glass, felt, or plastic seals at the edges and efficient latches that pull and seal the windows where they meet at the center. There are units that tilt in so that both inner and outer surfaces can be washed from the inside. The best new window units replace all parts of the old window, fitting straight into the building wall.

Even if all the windows have been replaced and still have the labels on them, you should still try them for ease of operation: the best windows of any type will bind and stick if they have been poorly installed. In an older building where the windows are part of the original installation, settling can affect their operation. A wood window that has shrunk or warped to any degree will not work smoothly. Move the sash up and down and check for gaps at the top and bottom, which would indicate some shifting, and remember to keep looking for cracked or broken glass.

Horizontal Sliding Windows

Another less common type of window you may come across is a horizontal sliding unit. Check for binding or tilting when opening or closing. If the handles are not installed in the proper place, one edge of the window can tilt up or down and cause the sliding section to jam in the track. The tracks for sliding units should be clean and free of dust and dirt—any extraneous material in the lower track will impede free movement and ease of operation. As with any other window, framing has to be level and plumb.

The better quality of horizontal sliding sash would be double-glazed in fairly heavyweight frames. Double glazing should eliminate the need for storm sashes. If there are storm windows, they also would be of a horizontal sliding type and with the same potential problems as the primary windows.

Many sliding windows are aluminum and, as with the aluminum storm windows, can become pitted and rough. Unless there are missing pieces of the metal framing, or holes eroded through the metal, cleaning and lubricating may restore the windows to a nearly new look. If windows of any type are anodized aluminum, the surfaces that are exposed to weather should be looked over carefully for wear or other damage to the surface coating. Vinyl-clad, wood, or metal units should be checked for surface integrity—bubbled or cut areas could cause the surface coatings to flake off. Any of the above windows may have screens. If they are not in place, you should find out if there are any, or you will have to buy them when you move in. Screens should be checked: Do they fit and do they operate freely? Look at the condition and finish of the screens themselves. Torn, patched, and loosely fitting screens will need to be replaced.

The screen fabric can be aluminum, plated steel or iron, copper, or fiberglass. The major concern should be the condition of the screening, rather than the material—unless there are rusted screens that appear ready to fall apart immediately.

Casement Windows

The last, but not least, common type of window you are likely to come across is the casement unit, either wood or metal. Newer housing or a building where older windows have been replaced may have units where wood- or vinyl-clad wood or metal is exposed to the weather. These newer units usually open and close by turning a crank at one lower inside corner. The window may lock by turning the crank tightly, or it may have an auxiliary catch along the rail opposite the hinge side. Look to see that the windows appear to be plumb and square, and by all means try them.

If the windows do not fit squarely, or if they have shifted for any reason, they will probably bind when they are opened or closed. They also may not fit smoothly in the latched position. Newer types of casement windows usually have screens that snap or otherwise fit the inside framing. If the building is going to need screens, you should make sure that they are available for the windows on the premises. You may face a problem in the future trying to find screens where latches or locks line up.

Most newer, large-paned casement windows probably will have insulated or double glass, so that storms are not needed. Some windows even may be triple-glazed, with two air spaces separated by glass. There are windows that have snap-in grilles to make the large glass look like small panes. If you encounter this type of window, you should try to determine if it is insulated glass—often units with small panes are not.

One of the problems with storm windows or screens for older casement windows is that they have to be fitted on the inside and are installed in tracks at the top and bottom of the inner window framing. All of them have to be made to order, and they are fairly expensive. If the frames that hold the glass or plastic are not fairly heavy and rigid, something will warp or twist out of shape. If there are inside storm windows or screens to the casement windows, you should definitely try them to make sure they slide without binding or lifting out of the tracks. Many inside sliding storm windows fit poorly where they meet in the center and present draft problems: Look for a good fit and for some kind of fabric seal, such as felt.

Old wood casement windows are not common, but there are many still being used. These would be the tall wood units with small glass panes that look much like French doors. These are usually heavy and ill-fitting. If you come across this type of window, check for drafts along the edges and where they meet in the center. Look carefully for rot damage at the lower edges of these windows, where they rarely get painted on the underneath parts of the lower rail. The wood windowsills to these units tend to suffer rot damage, probably because of their width and lack of pitch. The older wood windows never seem to have weather stripping or storm sashes—other than the old, heavy wood units that are hung on the outside.

Newer replacement wood casements usually come with narrower frames and with one insulated glass pane to each window. The replacements may have snap-in grids to give the appearance of the original small-paned unit.

With older windows of this type you should pay attention to the wood moldings that separate the glass panes. Check the condition of the putty that holds the glass in place. Check the fit of the windows in the frames by opening and closing them. Often what looks correct and tight when closed will prove to be warped when opened. Warped or twisted windows will have to be forced to close them, and the forcing will damage the frames or cause them to separate at the corners where they are joined. Poorly fitted, warped, or twisted units may need replacement at any time.

Steel casement windows can be found almost anywhere and in a variety of building styles. They may be in Victorian buildings where they were put in, perhaps in the thirties, as improvements. They may be found in buildings dating from the thirties as the original windows. You might find them in suburban or urban housing, small one-family units, or apartment buildings of any size. Steel casements are usually fastened at the top and bottom corners with a pivot hinge, rather than the hinge usually associated with a door. They are fastened shut with a pivoted handle that hooks over a center rail. Where there are a pair of windows in one opening, the handle hooks into a slotted opening in the frame opposite the hinged side. A much larger version of a casement window may be found as a door, usually at the side or rear of a building but not as the main entrance opening. When in pairs, very large metal casement windows and doors usually have a sliding latch at the top and bottom of one of the pairs. The latch pushes a metal tongue into holes at the top and bottom of the metal framing to make one door or window rigid. The other door fastens to the rigid one and both will be locked. You should check both doors and windows in this type of situation to make sure that the unit swings freely and does not drag or bind. Check that the center latch can be opened and closed with no effort when you want the larger opening. The door that is not used also should be tried to make sure that it really operates and that there is no problem with the hinges. Also make sure that it has not been permanently fastened. You should be very careful in checking casements, since even changing cracked or broken glass is very expensive. Because metal casements expand and contract more than wood, new glass must be accurately cut. You may find that glass tends to crack after a very long, hard winter. Temperature changes from 100° in summer to 0° in winter can mean many panes will need to be changed. You cannot tell what or where replacements will be needed, so check for what is a current problem.

There are any number of problems unique to metal casements. One of the more obvious is rusting. At the lower corners, where a unit has been neglected, the rust may eat away the entire lower edge or the corner where the pivoted hinge fits. If the pivot or hinge rail is gone, you may need an entirely new window unit. A heavy paint buildup over many years may make tight closing nearly impossible or, when a window is opened, may make closing difficult. Most older casement windows have adjustable slides to limit the size of the window opening, to keep the windows from swinging freely and damaging themselves.

Paint-filled slots, dirt buildup, or rust will make the slides unworkable in many cases. If the slide units are not rusted away or broken, cleaning and oiling will improve operation. Total replacement, if needed, may be a problem with older units, since it will probably be impossible to locate parts.

Where there are center slide latches, they should move with finger pressure and not have to be hammered. Oil or other lubricants may help; stubborn slides may be made to work easier by the use of penetrating oil. The condition of the paint on metal casements should be checked, since rust under the painted surface may become a problem. If there is a lot of rust or if pivot hinges or other parts are missing, you may have to replace an entire unit. With a wood window you might be able to replace a rotted wood section, but with metal casements the chance is very slim.

As you walk through any building you are thinking of purchasing, you should almost automatically be checking walls and ceilings for cracks, stains, or sagging areas. You should check for doors that do not fit closets or other openings. Look for framing around doors and windows that is out of line or tilted. Also look carefully at corners of framing for gaps or openings that have spread apart since the last painting.

Visual checks of any building or living area become almost automatic if you can block out checking furniture, wallpaper, and pictures on the walls. Carrying a notepad makes it easier to remember what you have seen and also enables you to list items you may want to question, or to list items that may or may not go with the property (appliances, air conditioners, etc.).

The Kitchen

Designs for older houses did not always make the best use of space, especially in the layout of kitchens. Traffic patterns between rooms or even getting from a kitchen to a dining room sometimes feels like it just happened, rather than was planned for. A closet door that opens and overlaps a door to another room may be an annoyance.

While in the kitchen you should try the water pressure at the sink and check to make sure the faucet works without any leaking where it connects to the sink. Look under the sink for any leaking pipe connections and to make sure the waste line does not leak when water runs through from the sink. Look for shutoff valves under the sink at the same time.

Cabinet drawers should be checked for ease of operation and to make sure they work without being forced. Cabinet doors should be checked for fit and to see if latches hold. Generally, cabinets should be checked for their condition, style, and age and probably for type: Are the cabinets a quality wood? Are they painted or covered with a plastic laminate such as Formica? You may know little about cabinetwork but you should be able to tell something of the quality of the cabinets by the way doors and framing are fitted and if the installation was done so that everything lines up.

Appliances cannot really be checked other than by using them. If you turn a stove or a dishwasher on and off you will only learn that they go on and off; I do not know any professional home inspectors that check appliances. You can get some idea of quality if you know brand names and which models are the top of a brand line, but guessing the age of many appliances is difficult. You might want to make a note of the names and model numbers of the appliances—stove, refrigerator, washer, dryer, etc. —to make sure they are still there when you close on your property. A stove may be gas-operated with gas supplied by a utility company or might work on propane delivered to the house in large tanks; it might be an electric unit; and if you are really off the beaten path, it could be wood- or coal-burning.

Look for a ventilating fan if there is no kitchen window and also check for a fan-operated stove or oven hood (this type of fan is to remove odors and not ventilate the kitchen). A stove or oven hood might vent to the outside or be a self-contained unit with washable filters; turn any hood on and off to make sure the fan and light, if any, works.

Kitchen flooring might be wood of any number of types, such as oak, maple, pine, or a combination of wood with another material. Flooring might be a one-piece resilient covering once called oilcloth or linoleum, and when very heavy and thick called "inlaid." The floor also might be a resilient tile that is glued to a subflooring of plywood or Masonite, or it might be a variety of ceramic tile. Whatever the floor material is, you should be looking at condition and looking for cracks or sunken-in sections.

So far we have covered the exterior of the property and have gone through the living area. Certain mechanical aspects and obvious structural problems have been looked into.

III.
The
Cellar

Now, as we move down to the cellar, observation can tell us about the basic structure of the building to give some insight into the major systems of the building. Most cellars, by definition, are below ground level. There are, of course, many buildings where everything pertaining to the building is on ground level and would be considered a basement.

A below-ground cellar might have small windows just above ground level or windows set below ground in window wells to provide some light and ventilation. As with other windows in the building, you should be looking at condition: Check the paint, look for rusted or rotted sections, and look for cracked or broken glass. If the window wells are protected with metal grates to prevent illegal entry, then look for rusted or badly deteriorated metalwork.

We are now interested in checking the heating plant of the building, water and other utility inlets, exposed wiring and plumbing. Since the majority of the cellars you will be looking at are below ground, one of the first things to look for is a convenient light switch at the top, or near the top, of the stairs. As you go downstairs you should be checking automatically the stability of the stairs—are they solid-feeling, and are treads and risers correctly spaced so that walking down is comfortable?

In older buildings, where the stairs may be very narrow and steep, or where they are curved, you should think ahead and try to anticipate what you may want to take up or down the stairs and try to visualize if it will fit. If you wanted to take a full four-by-eight-foot sheet of plywood or paneling to the cellar, could you do so? If you made a large picture frame or a piece of furniture, would you be able to get it up the stairs?

Where there is no below-ground cellar (as in a house built on a slab) and the heating plant, hot-water tank, washing machine, and other items are placed in areas no larger than closets, some thought should be given to maintenance access or even to how *you* would fit while doing washing or adding water to a boiler or draining water from a hot-water tank.

Cellar Floor

In a below-ground cellar, starting with the floor, you could find a dirt floor, concrete slab, resilient tiles, wood, ceramic tiles, or even brick. One of the most obvious problems you could encounter regarding

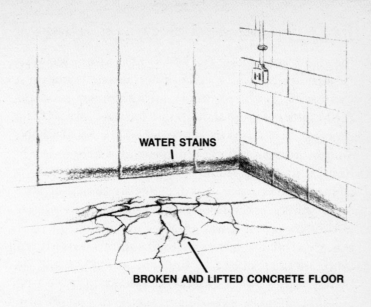

WATER STAINS

BROKEN AND LIFTED CONCRETE FLOOR

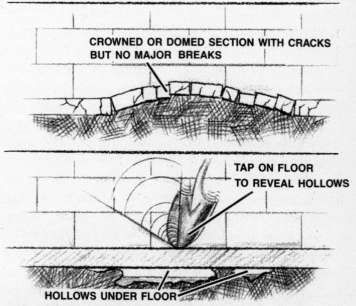

CROWNED OR DOMED SECTION WITH CRACKS
BUT NO MAJOR BREAKS

TAP ON FLOOR
TO REVEAL HOLLOWS

HOLLOWS UNDER FLOOR

Cellar floor problems shown up as broken, heaved up, or
hollow areas.

the floor would be cracks or heaved-up sections. Domed sections of a cellar floor usually indicate a hydrostatic problem where groundwater pressure pushes the concrete slab up in a localized area. If the concrete cracks, it is usually patched but not flattened and so the dome shape remains and is hollow. It will have a drumlike sound if hit. Where there is a groundwater problem under a cellar floor but little or no pressure, the floor may not lift but subsoil gets washed away and leaves a hollow under the concrete; this area will also have a drumlike sound if hit. It is a more subtle problem to find and usually would be bypassed by a buyer with no experience in inspecting a home, and an experienced inspector might also miss the problem unless he was aware of water problems in a neighborhood or normally walked around stamping lightly looking for a problem.

Less obvious signs of flooding or seepage are stained sections of floor or gray or white marks on smooth sections of floor; the marks are usually uneven and look like the high tidelines on a beach. If a cellar floor is covered with resilient tile and the tile is tight on a solid concrete slab, you may find white or gray marks along the edges or seams of the tiles. This is efflorescence and indicates seepage that is leaching mineral salts through the concrete. Seepage or other groundwater problems may occur at certain times of the year or after heavy rains: Exterior drains or dry wells may not be able to handle excessive amounts of rain, or there may be problems with a catch basin or sewer line in the street; in winter the ground may be frozen and a sudden heavy rain cannot be absorbed. There may be many solutions, but first you have to decide if you have a potential problem.

Dirt floors with seepage or flooding problems have a damp, wet, or musty smell, and there may be dark sections of floor that are always damp; there can be eroded sections of floor where the dirt has shifted or floated to a new position. Very wet floors or walls may have mildew growing somewhere; sometimes there is fungus growing that looks like fur because it is so thick. Roots or plants may be growing up through the surface.

In very wet areas or where there is flooding or seepage, wood cellar floors will usually show mildew damage and either visible mold or a damp, moldy smell. There may be obvious rotted, spongy, soft surfaces. Wood flooring placed over dirt may not always show obvious surface damage but very likely will have hidden damage to support beams or joists where they rest directly on the dirt. These same wood support members may be damaged even where there is no flooding problem, because of the moisture content of the earth or from condensation, which develops between a cold dirt floor and warm cellar air. Wood cellar flooring very often suffers from termite or other insect damage, in addition to the rot problems. If you fall in love with a building that has a wooden floor over earth, you can anticipate replacing the wood sometime soon. If you must have a wooden cellar floor, it should be over a solid slab.

Seepage or Flooding

Any evidence of water or water-related damage to the cellar floor will, of course, have to be corrected. Before any correction is attempted, the source of water must be determined, as well as the reason why it comes into the building. If water problems occur at specific times of the year because of spring thawing or a local stream or pond overflowing, you probably will need to install a sump pump. You should look for flooding or seepage evidence very carefully: An owner who is anxious to sell may not be totally honest.

Cellar Walls

A variety of materials could be used for cellar walls: brick, cinder blocks, or poured concrete. The walls may be rough stone or cut and fitted stone blocks. The walls may be covered with paneling, plaster, plasterboard, or other rigid surfacing materials. The wall covering may have been applied directly to the wall or to furring strips.

Where the cellar walls are covered with panels or plasterboard and the walls behind are not visible, look along the lower edges of the finished walls for staining: evidence of flooding or seepage problems. Chronic leakage situations will manifest themselves by marks or stains on the floor that resemble tide-

change marks or tree rings. Any old, badly neglected
cellar with freshly painted walls or floors should
arouse your suspicion.

Covered cellar walls may show evidence of mildew along the top or bottom edge, or where seams
of two panels meet. The support studding for interi-
or, finished walls also has a potential for insect
damage and/or rotting problems. As you look along
the lower edge at the floor line, you may get some
idea as to whether there is seepage coming through
the outside walls of the cellar. Often washed-in dirt
will come through a support wall and be deposited
along the lower edge of inside, covered walls and will
look like sand or heavy dust. Cluttered cellars with
cartons lying around or piles of newspapers are the
easiest to find leaks in: If everything is dry and there
is no damp smell, there is an excellent chance that it
always stays dry or, at the very least, has not had a
flooding problem dating back to the earliest newspaper!

Of course, uncovered cellar walls make visual
inspection easier. Any cracks are some cause for
concern and should be questioned. Even more so,
cracks that have been patched and reopened may
indicate serious structural problems.

Concrete block or brick walls should be checked
for opened joints and for areas where bricks or blocks
have shifted or settled unevenly. Cracks in a joint
indicate a problem with the wall's support footing.
Cracking that occurs through the brick or block
might indicate undermining of dirt below the wall
area in that section. Cracking or shifting problems
could show up in the same way in any of the build-

ing's structural walls: Long cracks in a cellar might carry through to an upper floor and show up in the walls in relatively the same position. Stairs or floors on the way up can be affected if there is a structural problem. Settling in a building should not go on forever, unless there is a very good reason for it, and that might be a structural fault.

Supports

Brick support walls may have problems, especially where high moisture and little ventilation exist. Ideally, exterior-faced brick should be used for support walls in buildings where a high moisture factor and poor ventilation reasonably can be expected. These two situations usually coexist in city buildings. As moisture accumulates, soft, unfaced brick will absorb water, and as it does, it becomes more absorbent and spongy. This deterioration will make the bricks appear to be "dissolving."

If you are looking at a building with brick structural walls, check for damp, wet-looking spots; look for discolored brick and for bricks where parts of the surface have flaked away, giving a "peeled" appearance. Painted brick walls may have the paint flaking and dropping off in small sheets where there is dampness behind. If the brick is in good condition and the paint tight and unbroken, you may find droplets of moisture on the paint surface, as if the wall is "sweating." This condition of surface moisture may show up more in winter, when the outside temperature is very low and the cellar is hot, and in combination with poor ventilation and no air exchange. If the walls show beaded moisture, you can safely assume there will be a problem with the structural integrity of the brick. If there is no apparent problem, you can probably head off that potential, simply by making some provision to ventilate the cellar area.

Bricks that show some deterioration may be reclaimed by cleaning them of loose and flaking material and cementing over the surface to make them level with the surrounding area. After repairs are made, ventilation must be provided, or deterioration will continue.

Many urban row houses have brick piers holding up a main center supporting beam. The same approach applies here as for the brick cellar walls. If you find badly deteriorated brick columns, you will either have to replace most or all of the brick or rebuild the entire column. You could build a form around the existing brick column and then fill it with cement. Another alternative is to replace the brick with a solid lolly column. You should anticipate having to do the work immediately if the damage is severe. You might be able to get the seller to take care of it, because if the center support beam drops, it can cause considerable damage to the internal structure of the building: in a typical row house the center can drop and displace stairs and cause considerable plaster and structural damage. As you continue looking for evidence of seepage, check the bases

MAIN SUPPORT BEAM

Shifted or damaged brick columns can cause main support beam to drop or shift.

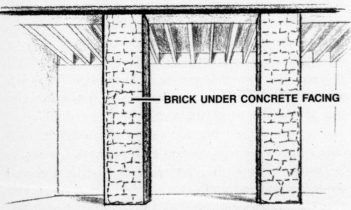

MAIN SUPPORT BEAM

BRICK UNDER CONCRETE FACING

Deteriorated brick columns can be cemented over for stability.

of columns or posts, or anything else that is vertical in the cellar—many times you will find water marks or rings where the water has stained something. Again, there may be what looks like tidemarks on a wall, door, or post.

Rough stone or "rubble stone" walls are fairly common and may be found almost anywhere, in any style of building. Many of these types of walls were put together with a mix that was mostly lime and sand, with very little mortar added. As the joints pick up airborne moisture in poorly ventilated cellars, the sand-lime mixture tends to fall out, leaving fair-sized gaps between the stones. Moisture or water from outside or from next door (in row houses) can and does push the mixture out. Because of the rough texture and oddly shaped stones used in this type of wall, shifting, movement, or cracking is difficult to determine. The easiest to locate is where a wall has shifted enough to bulge inward. Rubble walls tend to hold themselves together by being wedged in all directions, so that unless there is a large, bowed section, or an obvious gap and broken stone, the wall is probably sound.

If there are large gaps between stones, it might be a good idea to fill them, in an effort to eliminate one cause of shifting. If the gaps are in common party walls, as in row houses, filling the openings may also reduce the chance of rodents and insects coming from next door.

Cellar Ceiling and Supports

Cellar ceilings can be plaster, plasterboard, acoustical tile, metal, or wood, as well as any number of other things, including heavy cardboard mailing tubes. Many ceilings will be uncovered, and the ceiling joists and the underside of the flooring above will be visible. If the ceiling is not covered, you can get a look at the condition of the tops of support columns or posts where they meet the main bearing beam. If there is a finished ceiling, you are limited to a visual inspection of the surface and its general condition. Loose, broken, or missing sections of ceiling might indicate a possible leak, either of recent origin or possibly an old situation that has been corrected. Look around the damaged area for wet spots or active dripping. Look for any abnormality that might provide a clue to a problem. Holes that appear to have been cut, rather than broken, or that are around a cable, pipe, or wire, probably were made to allow access for repair or installation.

Of course, active dripping indicates a current problem and should be investigated further. If there is an active leak and visual access to the beams or joists around the leak, inspect the wood very carefully for rot damage or for highly saturated sections that might indicate a leak that has been going on for some time. A soft, wet beam with or without rot damage will have lost some of its load-bearing capability and structural integrity.

Stains on a covered ceiling might be an indication of a leak in a plumbing or waste line, or could have resulted from sink overflow. Only by opening the ceiling to some degree can you be sure where the leak is coming from. It is simpler to find leaks where the ceiling is uncovered and the joists exposed, but covered or exposed, the entire ceiling area should be checked.

Rot or Insect Damage

While still at the ceiling level and with screwdriver in hand, look over the ends of joists, where visible, and at the front and rear ends of the main bearing beam. Look carefully where they fit into pockets in the walls (or on sills or where the support members are fastened to any other support system). With your screwdriver poke the ends of the wood beams or any other suspicious section with a good deal of force: What you are looking for is evidence of either rot or insect damage. It is a good idea to make the same check where wood touches a floor, such as stair supports, posts, door framing, etc. Termites or other wood-destroying insects can show up nearly anywhere. The idea that termites do not appear in urban environments is totally wrong. Termites are not exclusively rural, and row houses can have as large a termite problem as a house in the woods. In addition to termites, there are carpenter ants and powder-post beetles, and who knows what else that can munch away at your potential investment. Rot

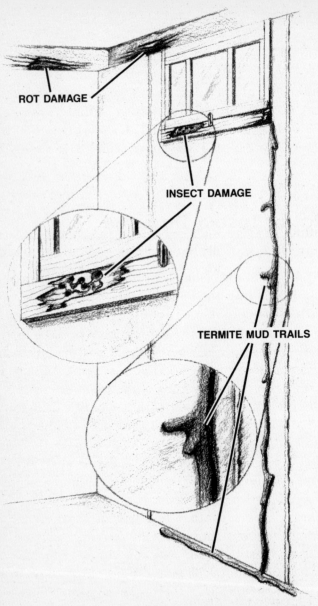

ROT DAMAGE

INSECT DAMAGE

TERMITE MUD TRAILS

Rot or insect damage can appear anywhere in the building, but most often in the cellar.

and termite damage look different if you have seen enough of both, but either is a traumatic discovery if you are thinking of purchasing a house, and an even more distressing discovery for an unaware seller if his potential buyer has just buried a screwdriver into the main beam and it only stopped because the handle got in the way.

Rot damage—and it does not matter if you call it wet or dry rot—is a direct result of water: either as an ongoing leak or a moisture problem, where wood cannot dry and water soaks into it rather than running off. Eventually the wood rots, and a nice, warm, wet cellar is the ideal place for both rot and insects. Often dry-rotted floors are found in buildings where the flooring has been covered with linoleum for years. Over the years the floor was mopped and a good deal of water ran under the linoleum. Since the water could not evaporate or dry in any way, it soaked into the wooden floorboards, causing a rot problem. Dry now, it is described as a dry-rot problem, but it started out wet. Running the toe of your shoe across the grain of flooring where linoleum has recently been removed may make the wood roll up in small patches that look almost like hair—that is one telltale aspect of a dry-rot problem. If the damage is mostly on the surface, the floor can probably be refinished and retained. If you have any doubts or any question, check with someone experienced with flooring, wood, or refinishing.

While poking around the beams and joists, look for termite mud trails or mud tubes: these are brown or beige to gray and are usually found on the outside surfaces of wood sections. Mud tubes act as tunnels and allow termites to move from place to place without being exposed to light. The tubes look like thick dust or dirt that has been squeezed out of a tube, not unlike a long squirt of toothpaste. The tubes vary in thickness and length and may run from one inch to several feet long. They may be about one-quarter to three-eighths of an inch thick. The tubes are not usually straight but may run on for a distance and then change direction. If you poke or scrape the tubes, they will crumble and fall apart, usually leaving a mark on the wood surface the same general shape and length of the tube.

Powder-post beetles or carpenter ants do not build mud trails but may leave more obvious evidence of activity, such as small piles of sawdust or powdered wood. If you have any suspicion of wood-destroying insects, first question the owner and/or broker, but by all means, if you continue to have an interest in the purchase of the building, have a qualified exterminator check the building and give you a written opinion.

In some areas of the country banks require a termite inspection as part of a mortgage commitment. It would be a good idea to have any building checked for termites even if you had no suspicion of any problem—and even if it is not a bank requirement—unless you are looking in an area that is guaranteed to be free of wood-destroying insects.

IV.
Heat, Water, and Power

Oil Storage

If you are looking at a building that is fueled with oil and the storage tank is in the cellar, look around the tank(s) for leaks, spilled oil, or oil spots on the floor near the tank. Look underneath the tank for dripping or seepage. Interior oil storage tanks occasionally get overfilled, and oil runs out and over the top and down the sides of the tank. Any evidence of oil outside the tank should be questioned.

An oil storage tank may be buried outside the building and not visible. Inspection of such a tank is not possible, and the owner may not even know where it is. In a suburban area it will be located in the front or side yard under the lawn. If there is a visible fill opening near the building, the tank is probably under it. Unless there is an oil slick on the lawn, or the lawn and tank have collapsed and sunk, you will not know its exact location. The oil company that supplies oil and service to the building may also provide tank insurance. If you have any concern about having to replace the tank, you should contact the oil company and get their opinion.

A multiple dwelling or a building that stores a large amount of oil might have a vaulted oil storage tank in the cellar. Local fire codes may require that anything over 550 gallons, or thereabouts, be stored that way, rather than in a freestanding tank. A vaulted storage tank looks like a large cement rectangle, which may have pipes protruding from the top or end. It will have a tube going to a gauge, and all you will be able to discover if you find it is whether there is any obvious seepage or leaking. If there is a crack that comes through the outer surface and there is an oil smell, by all means find out why.

There are many things to look for in the cellar of any building: all the basic systems are there, as well as the inlets for gas (if the building has the service), electricity, and water. There are buildings that do not have gas or use bottled gas. Some buildings will have a well to supply water. There are buildings with no central heating plant, either because individual apartments have their own heating unit or because the building has electric heat controlled in the individual rooms.

Waste System

For no reason at all, start with the sewer and waste system, which you will have to find and identify. The

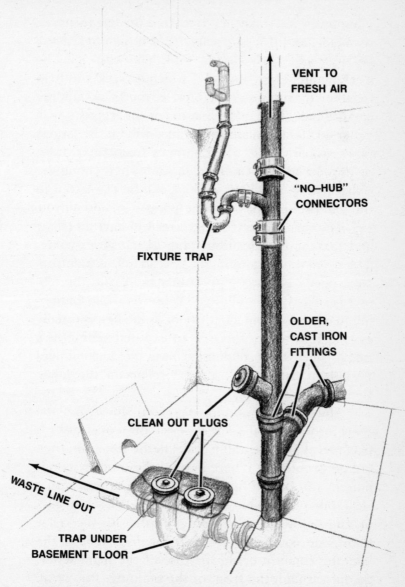

VENT TO
FRESH AIR

"NO–HUB"
CONNECTORS

FIXTURE TRAP

OLDER,
CAST IRON
FITTINGS

CLEAN OUT PLUGS

WASTE LINE OUT

TRAP UNDER
BASEMENT FLOOR

Typical waste system, partly cast iron, partly newer "no-hub."

main sewer lines may be three, four, or five inches in diameter, and if it is cast iron and unpainted, it will be rusty and fairly easy to find. The waste may be steel or the newer "no-hub," which is black and held together by shiny steel clamps. If the local building code allows, it may be plastic or fiberglass. As a general rule, the main sewer lines will be the largest pipes visible. Waste or drainpipes from sinks, tubs, or showers usually can be seen somewhere along the cellar ceiling, and they, in turn, will be connected to the main sewer lines at some point.

The waste lines from fixtures will have an elbow and may have a clean-out plug at the lower curve. The usual toilet waste might be lead and is identifiable as a curved, gray pipe. It may be plastic, though, or fiberglass where allowed. Waste or drain plumbing that comes from a bathroom or kitchen is usually easy to find where there is an exposed ceiling in a cellar, since most buildings have the kitchen and possibly a bathroom over the cellar on the lower floor of the house.

The main sewer pipe may run down into the floor and out to the street sewer or septic tank. It may run along one wall parallel to the floor and then out the front wall. Where most of the sewer system is buried, you should find either: a covered trap with a clean-out plug visible in a section of the sewer line, or one or two clean-out plugs flush with the cellar floor. The assumption is that the main systems of the building come in or, in the case of the main sewer, go out through the front of the building. Part or all of wiring, gas, or oil inlets, and possibly coal chutes (old or active), may come in through a side wall if the building is at the end of a row or a corner. Everything may come in or go out at the rear of a building where an alley serves as access for utilities. You will need to orient yourself to the entry area(s).

If the sewer line runs under the floor and you cannot see clean-out plugs or covers, the clean-outs may be in a pit under the floor and covered with a metal plate or a wood cover, either of which may be flush with the floor and have to be pried out to allow inspection. If the cellar is a finished area, the trap may be hidden under carpeting or tile. There should be some access to the main sewer clean-outs in case a sewer line ever has to be snaked out to the street main.

The main sewer line should have an "elbow" trap somewhere close to the clean-out plug and the wall where the sewer line goes outside the building. In a wall-hung or exposed sewer line, the trap will be U-shaped and dropped below the horizontal line of sewer pipe—past the trap, the sewer again returns to a straight line. If you remove the trap cover, you will find water at the bottom of the trap—this prevents methane gases from entering the building as the gases are generated in the sewer system. The wet trap also inhibits rodents from entering the building through the sewer system. Somewhere in the area of the trap and outlet you may find another section of heavy sewer pipe going up and out. This is either a fresh-air vent, again to expel gases, or a connection to a yard drain. In some cases you may find both.

Floor drain traps in a pit or flush with the floor

should have two visible covers, though one is not uncommon. The front is on the waste line that is the direct connection to the sewer, and the inner cover (the one away from the wall) is the same as the inner one on the exposed wall-hung sewer. Again, if the rear cover is removed, you should see water, since it is a wet trap and acts the same way as the wall-hung type to keep gases and rodents out of the building.

Where there are two caps over a sewer line and they are flush with the floor, the inner one can be removed to drain the cellar in case of flooding or a major leak. If water is coming up into the building through the sewer pit or through the covers on the waste lines, of course you would not want to open the covers at all, but flooding caused by groundwater or other seepage, such as a backed-up dry well or water coming through a wall, could be drained away by opening the cover. The front cover of the two should not be removed unless the main sewer line is to be snaked to the street. Under normal conditions all caps or covers on sewer pipe should be tight. Make sure there is a cover when you are looking over the waste system. If there is none, you may get a raw sewage odor or possibly water spraying out of the sewer line. Of course, buried sewer pipe makes a visual inspection impossible, so all you can do is to look over the area where the stack goes into the ground and check for damp spots. There may be more than one vertical waste stack, and of course, all should be checked.

If you can, you should try to follow along the path that the waste stack takes from the point that it goes underground to the front clean-out trap or pit. You may find a line of cracked, stained, or heaved-up floor, which might be an indication of backing up or leaking in the horizontal underground pipe.

Going upward from where the pipe enters the floor, check for any streaking or staining and for water, dampness, or wet spots, any one of which might indicate water running down the outside of the drainpipe. Depending on the type, age, and how the building was originally piped and how it was possibly altered, you might be able to check high up on the vertical waste stack. Sometimes, in altering a building, old air shafts or dumbwaiter chutes were used to run plumbing or wiring to the upper floors. If this is the case, then almost the entire length of the waste pipe may be exposed and, for that matter, plumbing risers and electric cable also.

Exposed sewer lines, or the exposed areas of buried ones, should be gone over carefully for leaking joints, obvious cracking, and sections that have been patched. Cast-iron sewer lines are the oldest type you are liable to encounter. You should check the joints for any seepage or backing up. Cast-iron sewer pipe is put together from sections of pipe that are straight, except for one end, which is bell-shaped. This, the hub end, has a straight section fitted into it from the next piece to be installed. When all the pipe has been put in place and supported oakum (hemp fiber) is forced into the joint, then molten lead is poured into the joint over that. You should be looking for lead that is not even with the edge, which might indicate some movement of the sewer system. This could be caused by outside vibration or because the pipe is not securely fastened to the wall. Lead that has moved only slightly can usually be pounded back into place.

Cracking or peeling flakes of metal may be caused by age and rusting in a damp cellar. Iron rusts on the inside of a pipe as well as on the outer surface, and so it can become very thin. Tapping the outside of a sewer pipe with the back of a screwdriver handle usually can give you some idea of how worn it is: a thin, flat, hollow sound would indicate a good deal of rust and wear; if you tap the hub, you will be able to hear the difference because of the hub's thickness.

Cracks or patching on a sewer pipe are fairly easy to identify. Cracks on the bottom or sides leak or drip, and the ones along the top are very obvious, showing up as opened splits. Any cracking will mean that that section of pipe will have to be replaced, and because all the sewer pipe was probably installed at the same time, it is very likely that another section may go at any time. Removing a section of cast-iron pipe is usually done by breaking it, which may, in turn, also crack another section, and that in turn may cause a third piece to break, and so on. It is not uncommon to have to replace half a sewer system because of one broken pipe section. This can be an expensive, initial repair for a new home owner.

Patched pipe can be an indication of a place that has rusted through, or if small, might be a hole that was intentionally made so that a snake could be put through. Whatever the reason, patching can indicate a problem. The type of patching might give some indication of the quality of repair: a screw-in fitting with a heavy rubber washer or a heavy clamp–type of patch, used with two sections of metal and screw fittings called a saddle (fitting) patch are the types that a good plumber might use. Such things as old window screen wrapped around the pipe and tarred over, or tar alone, or even roofing paper tied with wire and painted are more than likely to leak and require the replacement of that section of pipe. Now we are back to removing a defective section of cast-iron pipe and having to replace a good part of the main sewer line. Local building codes may not allow patching sewer pipe sections, and even if no leak develops, you might have to replace the pipe if a municipal building inspector sees it.

Defective sections of pipe can be removed easily in the newer no-hub sewer pipe (that is the black pipe with the shiny clamps). If replacement is required, it would be much less costly than the same amount of repair to a cast-iron system. No-hub pipe clamps are unscrewed and a new section of pipe clamped back together. Plastic pipe is impervious to anything short of a fire or being sawed through and should prove least likely to have any leakage problems. There might be seepage or dripping at a joint that was not properly connected. If a hole is made through the pipe accidentally, a section of pipe can be sawed out and a new section put in with the proper connectors. Plastic plumbing is put together either by threading it, as with regular pipe, or cemented with a solvent type of adhesive that melts or fuses the pipe in place. Plastic pipe or waste lines are not very common, and because of toxic fumes that will be produced if it burns, its use may not be permitted by local building codes.

Waste pipes that connect to tubs, showers, basins, etc. (but not to toilets), are much smaller than sewer lines, but all of them eventually end up in the main sewer of the building, either directly connected or through a vertical waste stack and then to the sewer line.

A waste pipe can be plastic, iron, or possibly copper, or it can be a combination of any of them. Look for leaking joints or connections and also for patched areas, which might indicate other problems in the plumbing or other systems of the building. As with the sewer lines, wastes may be patched with tarred rags, tape, or opened-out tin cans wired over a piece of rubber hose or inner tube. Rusting and/or dripping along a section of waste pipe would indicate a hole or crack. There may be pinholes or hairline cracks, and they may not be readily visible; but if there is rust and a wet spot on an otherwise clear section of pipe, the crack is there. Because waste or sewer pipe lines do not hold water at all times, except in their traps, the inside of the pipe(s) is normally fairly dry. Only when something is draining is the inner surface of the pipe wet, and even if there is a fair-sized crack, it may not drip all the time. If you suspect a leaking waste pipe, it would be a good idea to have someone run water into the fixture that connects to the suspect pipe and see if a drip starts when the fixture drains.

Leaking anywhere along a section of pipe usually means the entire length of pipe will have to be replaced to the next connection. Of course, a plastic pipe can have a piece cemented in. A copper waste pipe might have a new piece soldered in, using the correct fittings. The main waste system of the building may empty into a city sewer system, which would be the best and most trouble-free for you, the home owner. Where there is no city sewage, the waste will empty into a septic tank or, in very old housing or very rural areas, into a cesspool. You should be informed as to the location of the septic tank, and it should be on some type of map or other locator, so that it can be opened, inspected, and cleaned.

The tank and its access cover are both buried, and there is not normally any clue as to its location. If the cesspool or septic tank has not been checked or cleaned, you may be in for a very expensive repair or replacement. There are firms that specialize in the inspection, repair, and cleaning of septic systems. The system should probably be checked every two years or so. Overloaded or problem tanks are common where there is a dishwasher and washing machine, in addition to the regular waste system of a building. Each appliance should drain to a separate dry well. The local health department or the town engineer may be able to supply information on the tank problems in the locality concerned.

Another reason for knowing the location of a septic system would be so that you do not either dig the swimming pool where the tank resides or decide to build the spare bedroom extension over it.

Trees should not be planted in the area of septic tanks or cesspools, or along the area where the drain tiles run from the house to the tank. Where grass is very thick and richly green over the cesspool, you have a problem: either the unit is flooding, or full and overflowing. If you have a wet, spongy area on a lawn, and it is over a cesspool or a septic tank, you probably have a problem. I must stress this again: Have some knowledge of the location of the septic system and know when it was last checked and what the result was. If the check was longer than three to five years, you may be exposed to a big problem, either in repair or rebuilding bills.

Gas Pipes

Buildings with gas service will have a meter that should be easy to identify. It will usually have the name of the local utility company somewhere on the front and will also have several small dials with visible numbers. Finding the gas main should be no trouble, since it feeds into the meter and comes in through one wall, usually the front one. A pipe from the meter goes on into the cellar and through elbows and other connections; the pipe and the gas it contains end up at the appliances it fuels: stove, boiler, clothes dryer, or all of the above. Gas pipe is iron or steel, and a magnet will stick to it. Without a magnet you can just visually follow the gas pipe from the meter until it disappears up into the ceiling. Gas leaks usually occur because of a poor connection or where pipe thread has been cut too deeply. It is unusual to find a leak other than at a connection or shutoff valve—the valve itself may be defective. If there is a gas leak, you should be able to smell it—use your nose to locate the source of the leak. If you smell gas or even suspect a leak, do not light matches and put out your cigarette. The wisest approach would be for the owner or broker to call the local utility company or their favorite plumber. A gas leak can usually be found by mixing a little liquid detergent with water and brushing the mixture over pipe joints: a leak will cause a bubble to form.

Very small leaks, or leaks where there is no access to a pipe joint, can be found by the use of special meters or testers that a plumbing contractor, heating contractor, or utility company would employ. You should insist that the owner have any possible leaks checked out and repaired. As a new owner, you should not have the additional burden of a possible fire or health hazard to contend with.

Water Supply

Finding the water main coming into a building may take a little searching. The type of building, its age, and location are factors that might make the main's entrance into the building obscure. If there is a water meter, the main should be easier to locate. The main would normally come in through the front

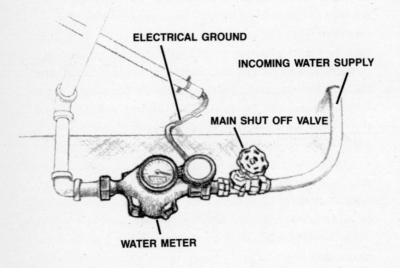

Most buildings have water meters at the water supply pipe from the street.

wall and probably near the gas main entry, if there is in fact a gas main, or in the area of a sewer line going out. The water main would be between the entry wall and the water meter. Newer buildings, or those that have been upgraded or maintained, are normally lit around the entry area of pipe and cable, and finding a particular element is not difficult. Problems usually occur in very old urban areas where a water main may come in around what was an old coal chute and is surrounded by old tires, a partly rotted mattress, or worse.

Sometimes a water main and its shutoff valve may be hidden behind a mass of pipe or electric cable, or may be behind a paneled wall or in a cabinet. If you cannot find it, you might ask the owner of the building. Often the owner will not be on the premises when you are checking a building, and the broker probably will not know where anything is—so you should try to find everything for yourself.

The type of water main coming into a building can vary and would depend on the age of the building and whether the building has ever been upgraded or renovated. Where local codes permit, a water main could be plastic pipe, or there might be plastic pipe from a well, or a storage tank connected to a well. The local water supply might be of such mineral content that copper or brass pipe is damaged or destroyed quickly. In that case, the main and all internal plumbing is, or should be, iron or steel. Usually water mains are copper, brass, iron, or plastic. It is not likely that you will come across a hollow wood log as a water conduit, but you might find the next type of pipe in the plumbing progression, and that would be lead.

A lead main is fairly simple to identify. For one thing, it is not magnetic, but then neither is copper, brass, or plastic. It is gray, but steel or iron can also be gray and both of them attract a magnet. Lead is, in addition to being gray and nonmagnetic, fairly soft, and you can shave off slivers with a knife, using very little pressure. Shaving will expose a shiny new surface that looks like silver.

In older inner-city housing you may, in addition to a lead water main, come across other sections of pipe, long lengths, or an entire water system of lead. If the building is old enough to have had lead plumbing, you should check carefully in the cellar. Even if what you see is new copper or brass, there may still be lead risers or lead connections to fixtures on the upper floors. Unfortunately you cannot see into closed walls to determine what the risers are made of. If lead plumbing is intact and not leaking anywhere, and if the joints where the lead and other metals meet are not leaking, you can probably leave the lead plumbing. When and if you upgrade the plumbing, you will probably have to replace all the lead with brass or copper. As a rule, plumbers do not like to work with lead and new, younger ones may not know how to. Modern fittings and parts do not blend into or with lead without a good deal of work. The lead water main can probably be retained unless it develops a leak.

If other pipe in the building is replaced, you might be advised by a plumber to replace the main at the same time. The inside of the main, and almost any other pipe in a water system, gets coated with whatever is the prominent mineral in the water supply, so water is essentially running through a calcium or limestone tube. If you have any concern about drinking water coming through a lead pipe, or any other plumbing, for that matter, you should have a water test made to determine mineral and/or bacteria levels, which will show if the levels of lead or copper are safe for drinking. With all the recent publicity about dump sites and the irresponsibility of the people who use them, it might not be a bad idea to have water safety tests done.

The next type of plumbing pipe to come along after lead was galvanized iron or steel, both of which have a common problem in that they rust. Both will rust externally in a damp, humid cellar or underground, unless coated to keep the pipe from direct contact with the ground. Both types also rust internally and, between the rusting and mineral buildup, lose the capacity to carry water, which means that in a very short time the water pressure in the building will drop. Unless the type of water in a particular area has an adverse effect on brass or copper and you must use iron pipe, you can anticipate the need to replace the iron at any time. Any questions you might have pertaining to how water and plumbing interact can probably be answered by the local water company, the town engineer, or the local building department. If an iron water main is mandatory, then go to a totally iron plumbing system. If plastic pipe can be used in your particular locality, it would be a better alternative than iron, because plastic will not be affected by minerals or chemicals. Iron and steel plumbing will attract a magnet, and you can follow a water line or iron plumbing from its entry into the building, or from a water meter, throughout the cellar, until it disappears up into a ceiling. Do not confuse gas pipe with water pipe as you are tracing it along.

While locating the plumbing lines you should also be looking for leaking joints, dripping valves, and rust or dripping along the length of the pipe. If you find the entire cellar or building piped with iron, you should check with the local water or building department to see if the water condition requires it. Either way, given the life expectancy of iron pipe, you can probably anticipate replacement of pipe sections periodically.

When the use of iron plumbing is not mandated by water conditions, and you find that most or all of the plumbing in a building is iron, you can assume that it was put in because the cost of iron pipe was considerably less than brass. Where threaded pipe and fittings were used, the labor cost was probably the same.

Under average or normal water conditions the most usual and longest-lasting water main is copper. At its entry point into the building, the copper main—or any other, for that matter—should be connected to a main shutoff valve. The valve in a copper line should be brass or copper. It is better to have two main shutoff valves should one fail to hold. If there is a water meter, the shutoff valve should be between the meter and the entry point into the building.

The brass or copper main past the shutoff valve and the water meter (if there is one) should then go to a brass or copper section of pipe, usually running just under the cellar ceiling. This pipe is called a reservoir. All other branch plumbing to risers, water tank, boiler, etc., should also be copper or brass.

Shutoff valves should also be brass or copper. Brass pipe is usually threaded together and connects to various threaded fittings, elbows, unions, etc. Copper or tubing is soldered, and the fittings, while the same style and type as for brass pipe, are also soldered and are lighter and not as thick. As with any other type of plumbing, look for leaking valves or connections.

If you have any doubts about the type of metal used, check with the magnet. At times a brass or copper pipe will turn black and may appear to be steel or iron—again, scraping will give you a second test.

One very important reason for checking all the plumbing, especially with a magnet, is that often an iron fitting or section of iron pipe is put into a brass or copper plumbing system with the result that galvanic action will rot or rust the iron where the two metals meet. Plugs, caps, and fittings, as well as the lengths of pipe, should be checked. Older buildings that have had many plumbing repairs, where standard-sized threaded fittings have been used, are the ones where you are liable to find the most problems. Either the repairs were done by a handyman who had no knowledge of the electrolysis problems that come with mixed plumbing or iron was used by the repairer because it was cheaper than brass. If a reliable, competent plumbing contractor mixes iron and brass in a water system, you almost feel it was done to perpetuate the repairs that such a practice would create.

There are special connectors made so that iron

or brass, or iron and copper, can be used in the same water system. These are made with an inert material between two metal sections; never having seen one in actual use, I would assume that they are difficult to find or that plumbers have no knowledge of them. Brass or iron plumbing are both cut to fit from long lengths of pipe, and then the ends are threaded so that the plumbing can be screwed together, using standard fittings. Because the threaded end of the pipe becomes very thin, it is important to check the parts of pipe that fit into other parts for seepage or dripping.

Copper tubing comes in rigid, straight lengths or in very flexible coils; local building codes will vary as to whether one or the other is acceptable within their jurisdiction, or if both can be used. Rigid tubing is soldered together, and local building or plumbing codes might require that a certain type of solder be used—though who checks it, or how the type would be determined after the work is done, is a moot point. Where rigid tubing is soldered, flexible tubing can be soldered or, more usually, put together with screw-in units called compression fittings. The two types of tubing are easy to identify, since in the rigid one, piping is done using straight sections and angles, whereas in flexible tubing the copper is just bent or curved wherever it has to go. Where work or renovations have been done in a building without a permit, or where haphazard repairs or other work has been done without supervision or conformation to the local building code, you may find any mix of materials and any quality of workmanship—from superior to bizarre.

Quality disparity might pertain to any part of a building but seems to show up more frequently with plumbing. Plastic pipe only requires a saw and a container of adhesive, which permits anyone to become an "instant plumber." Plastic pipe is one of the newest materials, and its use may be restricted to certain types of housing and in special applications. Again, use is controlled by local plumbing or building codes. As a do-it-yourself material, there is no code and no restriction, but when you find a section of plastic pipe epoxied between an old piece of lead and a threaded brass pipe, with black electrical tape wound around both ends, you get the feeling that a good deal of liberty has been taken.

Water from a well normally will supply a varying quality of water, depending on the locality and the various minerals in the supply. The amount of water may also vary depending upon the well's source of water, and may drop off in times of drought, or even in winter if there is a hard freeze. Heavy rust stains in a sink or tub, or with copper, which can cause green staining, would indicate water with a corrosive action. The water may have a metallic or other alien taste to you: holding a glass of water to the light might show suspended sediment. Well water should be tested or approved by the local water authority or by an independent laboratory. If you have any reservations about any water supply, you probably should have it tested, even if it is supplied by a city water system: the cost is moderate; for peace of mind, cheap.

A dug well is usually around twenty-five or thirty feet deep at most and has a top-mounted suction pump. A drilled well may be any depth beyond that and can be several hundred feet deep with a submerged pump or with a motor and pump system in a separate well house. The deeper well should be less affected by surface conditions or seepage or contaminants, but this would not be any guarantee of better water quality. While checking the visible condition of pumps or fittings and looking for leaks, you should also listen for any noise that the pump might make when it starts or runs.

Listen for banging pipes or even a low-level rumble or other noise: You will have to live with any noise you hear, and in other parts of the building there may also be vibration that you find annoying. Running the water simultaneously at several faucets throughout the building should give you some indication of the water pressure and possibly the drop-off or recycle time of the pump. With a well supply there may be a storage or holding tank for water, which should be checked for leaking, rust marks, and rusty or leaking fittings.

The local water board, town engineer, or building department might be able to give you information on water supply problems, such as seasonal changes, the mineral content of water, or its quality. There may be a water filter or water softening unit in the cellar for any type of water.

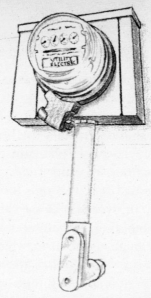

Electric meter may be in the cellar or outside the building.

Electrical System

Unless the building you are looking at is powered by a windmill or a waterwheel, you will have electric power coming into the premises that is supplied by a local utility company. The main cable will be either an underground installation or cable strung along a series of poles running up and down a street, with a connection to each building along the way. Either way, both will go through a meter that determines the amount of power you use, and thereby the cost to you.

If there is an overhead cable coming into the building, you should look for tree branches that are possibly going to interfere or sway into the cable in a heavy wind. Overhead electric cables should be high enough so that they clear trucks or other equipment that may have to pass under them. There may be a local regulation that determines the height. Check to see that the cable does not rub against, or come into contact with, chimneys or other rigid, rough surfaces that may abrade or break through insulation. There should be a loop or drop where the cable enters or is fastened to the building. If rainwater runs down the cable, it should run along the drop, which is U-shaped, and drop off rather than follow the cable into the building or through a covering pipe into the fuse or breaker box.

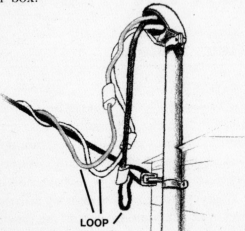

LOOP

Overhead power lines should have a loop to prevent rain water from following the cable into the house.

Somewhere around the meter or the main fuse box or main breaker box, you may find a square junction box: this is where the cable from the street is tied into the house electrical system. If there is no visible junction box, the cable may be connected in an outside box or may feed into the back of the main circuit breaker or fuse box. The thing you should be looking for around the junction box is rust. Where there is an underground cable installation—especially in older areas—the cables coming into the building are not always correctly sealed or packed, and water can follow the cable from a manhole in the street into the building. Most of the time you will find that the junction box is sealed and you will not be able to open or get into it. If there is a problem, rust on or around the box will be obvious. If there is an ongoing leakage problem, the box may be wet or even dripping. It is not improbable to find junction boxes with holes rusted through or with no bottom at all.

Usually the local utility company should repair any problem up to the breaker or fuse box in a building. They own the meter(s) and the junction box, as well as the cable and the wires to the box. The utility company may require that an electrician make the complaint to them if there is any question or problem. If you have any questions or doubts about the service line or the line's entry into the building—or, for that matter, anything—you should bring it to the attention of the building owner or broker. Any rust around the entry of the electrical service line into the building should be suspect.

While you are looking around the electrical main and its entry cable, look for a heavy wire or cable that comes out of the main fuse or circuit breaker box and is connected to the water pipe where it comes

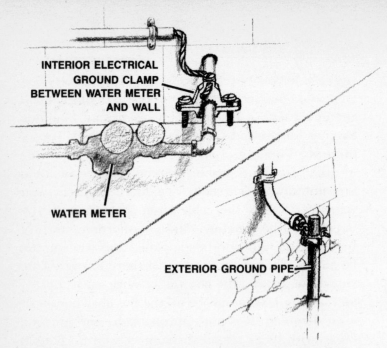

INTERIOR ELECTRICAL
GROUND CLAMP
BETWEEN WATER METER
AND WALL

WATER METER

EXTERIOR GROUND PIPE

All electrical systems must be grounded to the cold water pipe with a clamp, or directly to the ground on a pipe.

into the building. If there is a water meter, the connection of the cable should be between the meter and the wall. The cable should be tightly fastened with a screw clamp. This cable is an electrical ground, and unless it exists and is tight, the entire building can be a potentially lethal shock hazard. This ground is required nationally in any permanent structure.

When there is no underground water pipe, or if the length of pipe between the wall and a water meter is too short for a clamp, or if the water pipe is plastic, then the electrical system is grounded by a cable being fastened to an iron rod that is buried in the ground. You should be able to find the top of the rod where it comes out of the ground, then follow the ground wire from the electrical box. Outside, buried rods would be connected with wires or cables coming from the building. There may be a lightning rod on top of the building, and this is also connected by a wire or cable to a rod, which is also buried in the ground.

The electrical service, or the power coming into the building, is determined by the size of the cable from the street. This main power source into the building should be fused in the main fuse or breaker box, but there may be a smaller, separate box that contains the main fuse, and this, in turn, would be connected to the main box containing the fuses or breakers for the branch circuits.

The main fuse for the building might be a cylinder-shaped "cartridge" fuse. This is held in clips by the metal ends of the fuse itself; the clips that hold the cartridge fuse in place might be round to conform to the round end of the fuse, or where the fuse ends are flat, the clips will be shaped like a slot. It is more likely that the main fuse will be one with slotted ends, since the round-end type is for lower power. The more familiar fuses are the smaller, round screw-in glass or porcelain ones with a small window on the back, which indicates if the fuse is good or has blown. A small, screw-in fuse used on the main power source for the building would indicate a grossly underpowered structure. The main fuse for the building might be a small black box with a handle at the rear end; this is called a fuse block and contains two knife-edge cartridge fuses. The capacity of the fuses may or may not be marked on the block itself.

Most controls used for new residential electrical systems would be circuit breakers. Circuit breakers look like small switches, and there is a type that looks like an oversize push button. Look in the main junction or breaker box and try to determine the power coming into the building. There may be an amperage rating marked on the main fuse, main breaker, or on a plate or label attached to the door of the box. The rating is marked for 30, 60, or 100 amperes or more and may also be marked 120, 240, 440 volts, or more.

The amount of power coming into a building, and what you may need, can be vastly different. If the building you are interested in was built in the last five to eight years or so, it very likely has sufficient

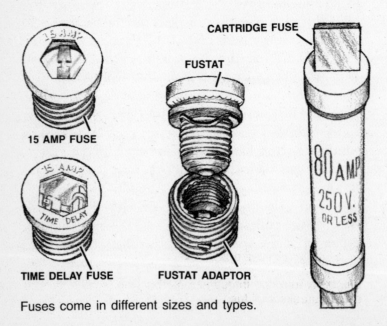

15 AMP FUSE

TIME DELAY FUSE

CARTRIDGE FUSE

FUSTAT

FUSTAT ADAPTOR

Fuses come in different sizes and types.

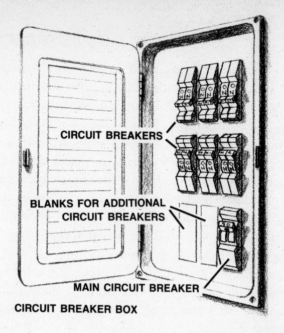

CIRCUIT BREAKERS

BLANKS FOR ADDITIONAL CIRCUIT BREAKERS

MAIN CIRCUIT BREAKER

CIRCUIT BREAKER BOX

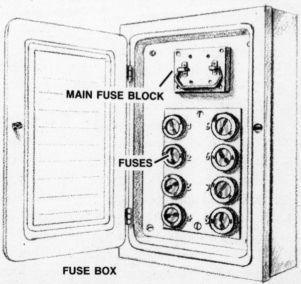

MAIN FUSE BLOCK

FUSES

FUSE BOX

Electricity into and throughout the building is controlled by curcuit breakers or fuses.

power and outlets for most appliances. A one- or two-family dwelling should have a minimum of 100 to 150 amps, 220 volts coming into the building as the main electrical supply. A very small building could probably get on well with a 60 amp, 220-volt main.

A building with electric heat would need much more power coming in than a building with a gas or oil-fueled heating system. In an older urban or inner-city dwelling you might find the newest wiring, with new circuit breakers and all the cable or conduit laid out as straight as a draftsman's drawing. Or you may encounter horrors that include open junction boxes with hanging, live wires; B.X. cables in water that are partially rusted through; missing or disconnected electrical grounds, and thin lamp cord wired into boxes with bare connections. It is not uncommon to find a 15- or 30-amp main fuse for an entire building, and only one or two outlets for an entire floor. You may find deadly fire hazards where aluminum foil has been wrapped several times around a cartridge fuse.

One building—a prime candidate for total destruction by fire—had a piece of copper tubing as a main fuse, instead of the normal cartridge fuse it should have had.

In many buildings the electrical systems have never been upgraded for twenty to fifty years. In all probability these buildings should be totally rewired and will need a new main service line brought in from the street. If extensive rewiring, additional wiring, and/or a new service has been installed in the last five years, the electrical system is probably adequate.

Ideally, a room should contain an electrical outlet where needed. In a new building you may find one every eight or ten feet, whereas in the older structures where no electrical work has been done (other than adding extension cords), you may only find one outlet on each wall. Often there is only one in each room or none at all. There are many buildings, built prior to the thirties, where outlets are high up on a wall or built into a ceiling light fixture or wall sconce.

There is a certain amount of confusion that centers around 220-volt outlets. Appliances that require 220 volts are: electric stoves, large electric dryers, very large air conditioners, or heavy, industrial-type machinery. There are, of course, other things that require 220 volts, but they would be clearly marked. Confusion stems partly from the assumption that an outlet with three holes, or a plug with three prongs, is used for 220 volts. Most plugs for items such as lamps, radios, and televisions have only two prongs, and, being most familiar, are commonly accepted as 110-volt users.

The usual 110-volt outlet has two parallel slots; the plug has two parallel prongs. Both are flat, and if the outlet is relatively new or has been upgraded, it also will have a small, round opening to receive the round prong. With newer, three-prong plugs, the round prong fits into the round hole in the outlet and grounds the appliance, thus lessening the chance for electric shock.

220-volt plugs are larger than the ones you usually handle, and so therefore are the outlets that receive them. The prongs on the plugs are angled, as are the slots in the outlets: they are not parallel and are designed and spaced so that 110-volt plugs will not fit. If a 110-volt appliance or tool could somehow be plugged into a 220-volt outlet, it would overheat, smolder, and probably burn. Or the item might explode before the fuse blew or the breaker switch was tripped. By the same token, a 220-volt plug cannot fit into a 110-volt outlet because of the size difference. If it could, the 220-volt item would operate very slowly or might not move at all.

Checking the electric meter in a building might give some indication of the power potential. A meter marked three-wire (3) would normally indicate a 220-volt service line into the building. Labels inside the door or covers of fuse or breaker boxes usually give the power rating. Counting the number of fuses or circuit breakers would give you some idea of the number of separate circuits in the building. There should be one for general lighting in an area; heavy-use appliances or fixtures should have their own circuit.

Unfortunately, few boxes are marked to indicate what is controlled by which fuse or breaker. If by chance they are labeled, there is, of course, less confusion. Generally, any major appliance should have its own separate circuit: a boiler should have its own breaker or fuse, and a central air-conditioning system should also be separately fused from other items. Washers, dryers, attic fans, and workshops need to be controlled separately. If you have more separate circuits, fewer items are on the same line

and there is less likelihood of tripping a breaker or
blowing a fuse because of an overload. Other than
the visual inspection and using the observations just
made, you either would have to be especially knowl-
edgeable about electricity, or you would have to
remove the cover of the box and measure the incom-
ing voltage with a meter or measure the same incom-
ing voltage across the connecting terminals of a main
fuse.

Around the mid-sixties, aluminum wire came
into widespread use, and with it came many problems. One of the worst occurred when aluminum
wire was connected to outlets and switches that were
designed for copper wire only. The problem with the
connections was, and is, that unless the wire is connected very tightly, there is a possibility of sparking,
overheating, or an oxidizing effect, which can break
the wire or cause it to start a fire. At times you can feel
heat around a switch or outlet plate if you place your
hand flat against it. The only sure way to tell if wire
or cable is aluminum is to remove the cover plate
from the switch or outlet and visually examine it.
Aluminum is, of course, silvery-looking, while copper looks like a penny. Removing the cover of the
breaker box will show what the various wires going
to outlets or switches are made of. If you do remove
the cover from the main circuit breaker box and find
that the feeder wires are aluminum, you will then
have to go on to remove the cover plates from
switches and outlets to see if they are the type
suitable for aluminum wiring. Both should be marked
for suitability. An aluminum main coming in from

the street or an overhead pole does not create a problem.

If you find that the outlets and/or switches have aluminum wire and that they are not the type of unit that is made to accept aluminum, you will have to have an electrician connect copper wire connectors using special crimp-on fasteners. This type of repair can be expensive, but certainly less so than a fire. Given the tendency of aluminum to cause problems, it might be a good idea to have the copper added, even if the outlets could take aluminum. If you have any suspicion, ask questions.

Where flexible "Romex" cable is used, you should be able to read the stamping on the surface. It should be clearly marked, either copper or aluminum. Unfortunately, B.X. cable or wire molding will not allow this. If you have any hesitancy or fears about removing outlets or the main breaker box cover, you should have an electrician or other expert do it for you. I cannot stress enough: Aluminum wiring has caused fires and extensive damage to buildings.

Hot Water System

Another major item that you will find in many cellars is a hot water tank to provide domestic hot water. Unless your boiler has a tankless coil, you will find a tall cylinder-shaped unit somewhere, probably near the boiler. A hot water tank can be fueled by gas, oil, or electricity. The capacity of the tank, as well as its recovery rate, will normally be found on a printed plate somewhere on the unit. A small house might need a tank no larger than twenty or thirty gallons, while a four-story, two- to six-family unit might need a seventy-five- or even a ninety-gallon unit. Where there is an existing hot water tank, you may assume that it is the correct size for the building, but since needs vary, it may not prove to be so.

Your major concern at this point, however, should be whether the unit is in working order. There is a drain valve at the lower end of hot water tanks; opening this valve and draining it slightly can give you some idea of how well maintained the tank is. You should get no more than one half to one cup full of dirty water before the water starts to run clear. You must be careful when draining a tank, because the water is very hot and may scald you. At times the drain valves are very tight or even rusted shut; if that is the case, it should not be forced, because it may break off, or you may not be able to close it. If you do attempt to open the valve, place a container under the spout to catch the water.

If you get more than a cup of dirty water, or if the water is rusty, there may be a leak inside the tank. There should be a pressure-relief safety valve at the top or topside of the tank. This is usually a valve or angled piece of metal connected to what looks like a stubby pipe. It may or may not have a thin metal piece that looks like a small handle, and there may or may not be a thin pipe connected to the valve and reaching or pointing toward the floor. Place a container under the outlet of the safety valve and carefully lift the finger piece—it should work very easily without the need for pressure. This will allow some water to drain out and, again, will give you some indication of rust inside the tank. A little dirty water is normal. This test will also confirm that the valve is in working order.

As with the lower drain valve, you should get about a cup of dirty water from the top blow-off valve if the tank has no leaks, and if it has been drained from the bottom on a regular basis. It is possible that the water will be clear, with no sediment and no rust. Again, be very careful when opening the valve—the water will be very hot, will come out with a good deal of force, and may spray. If the valve does not move or open easily, or if no water comes out, then the valve probably needs to be replaced. Check the plumbing connections to the tank for dripping or seepage. Look over the body of the tank for rust streaks and check along the top cover seam for rusting or leaks. Look for rust or wet spots at the bottom or under the tank: removal of the front access cover will allow visual inspection of the lower and inner section of the tank. Again, look for rusting and leaking. This type of checking procedure may be used for any type of tank, regardless of its fuel: gas, oil, or electricity.

Heating Plant

The major item in the cellar is the heating plant for the building. This may be oil- or gas-fired (or possi-

bly coal, though these are rare today). A building
with electric heat usually will not have a central
location but is controlled by units in individual rooms
and with thermostats either in the same room or
close by. There may be an electric furnace, usually in
areas where heat is not needed on a regular basis—
such as the Deep South—or in areas where electric
power is cheap.

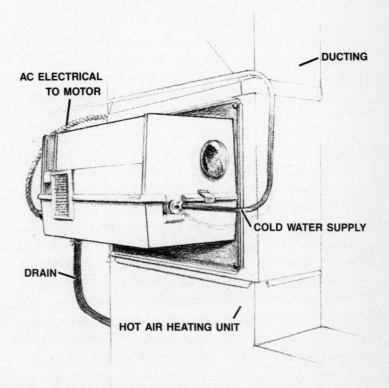

A humidifier adds moisture to a hot/forced air system.

Gas- or oil-fired heating plants can be steam systems, circulating hot water systems, or forced or gravity hot air types. A hot air unit will often have a humidifier connected to, or built into, it. The humidifier is usually a very small unit, about three by eight inches or one foot square, made of plastic and metal. A humidifier should be easy to find if there is one—look for the box-shaped unit attached to the side of the heating plant, or look for a thin copper tube connected to, and running from, a cold water pipe toward the heating plant, and you should find the humidifier at the end of it. In any case, check the point where the water valve is connected to the water pipe; make sure it is on and that it does not leak. Older, smaller humidifiers have covers that lift off easily, and you can see a float, which looks like a frosted light bulb. Normally, if the unit is working, the float will be in water, and if it is pressed gently into the water, the unit will start to fill itself. If there are rust streaks, rusty water, or holes in a humidifier, it probably needs to be replaced. If it is dry or water will not run in, or if the float is missing or broken, the unit will probably need replacement. Newer, larger units made of plastic will allow you to see the water and how clear it is. There may be various types of controls or gauges but the same type of filling arrangement. Newer units will usually have a drain valve, to flush and clean the unit. Again, if you have any doubts or questions, ask the owner or broker until you are satisfied and understand the working condition of the unit.

As to the hot air heating plant itself, it can be a

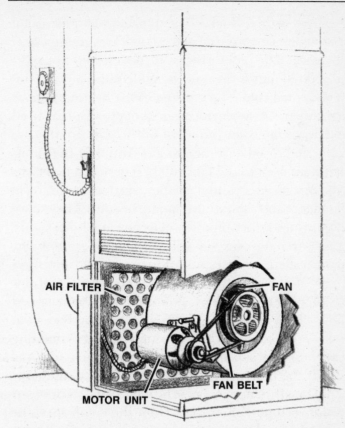

A hot air furnace with a fan is more efficient and newer than a gravity system.

fan-forced unit, where the heated air is circulated or pushed through a system of ducts with the assistance of a fan, which is, in turn, controlled by a separate switch or heat sensor. In older units the heated air is circulated by the principle that warm air rises and that as it rises, it is displaced by colder air, which is then heated as it comes back to the heat source through return ducts. The fan-assisted unit is, of course, more efficient and allows for greater heat dispersal. The older gravity system created hot spots in a room, mostly around the outlets and left the rest of the room cold. Some of the oldest heating systems are hot air. Many of the original ones were coal-fired and were later converted to oil or gas. Some were converted to oil and then to gas. You may find units that date back to the late 1800s. These original units are very large, cylinder shapes, six feet or more in diameter and about the same height. They have large, round duct pipes coming out in all directions. If you ever see one, you will quickly understand why it was called an "octopus." These very old units are made of galvanized tin or thin, sheet steel, and few of them were insulated. None of the originals had fans. These units are a drain on a heating budget at today's fuel prices. If you are interested in a building with one of these relics, you should figure into the cost of the building the cost of a new heating plant.

The efficiency of a new heating plant, as opposed to the "octopus" and apart from the comfort of the heat delivery, should pay for the new unit in a relatively short time. Many older hot air systems were not provided with return ducts to allow fresh, cooled air back into the cellar. Sometimes a floor return is covered with a rug. The absence of ducts, or the fact that they are partly covered, reduces the efficiency of any hot air system and makes the unit work harder than necessary. Fan-forced hot air systems all have, or should have, filters. These have to be replaced, as they get very dirty during the heating season. The filters may need replacement every four weeks. Washable and reusable filters are available, but the mess, as well as finding the proper place to clean them, may not make their use attractive to most people. If you have a large hardware or wholesale distributor in the area, you can probably buy a case of filters for less than the bothersome reusable ones. Checking the filter condition and cleanliness should give you some indication of the maintenance of the plant. If you cannot find the filters easily, ask the owner.

Fan-forced units may have a blade unit fastened on a shaft and turned by a belt connected to a motor. Or the fan may be a cylinder-shaped unit either running off a motor shaft and providing direct air, or it may also be a belt-driven unit. With the fan housing cover off and without touching any operating or moving parts, you can listen for squeaks that might indicate a need for lubrication or a slipping belt. Tapping or an uneven sound might indicate a bad bearing or a worn shaft, or just a worn belt. Even though you are not an expert, you should be able to hear any sound or noise that does not "feel" right: a well cared for unit should run smoothly and evenly, with no odd noises. With the unit turned off and with the emergency switch off, you can check for a worn or frayed belt, or one that is slipping on a pulley or drive wheel. Dirt accumulation around the fan or motor indicates poor maintenance and possibly an upcoming repair or service bill. You should question anything that appears strange, out of the ordinary, or that you do not understand.

A hot air heating unit, as stated earlier, can be

fueled by electricity, gas, or oil, but other than a visual inspection and turning on the unit to see if it works, you will not be able to tell much more unless you have had some experience with heating plants.

Gas-fired units have a small housing and a series of valves, and other than a low "whooshing" sound when the flame goes on from the pilot and the running of the fan, you should hear very little. As the unit heats up, you may hear creaking or a light, tinny sound where ducts or other metal expands or moves.

Older gas units have small motor housings at the burner location, with small doors or shutters that open and shut as the heat goes on and off. Have someone turn the thermostat on if it is off (or off, if it is on) and check the motor unit for smooth operation and for noise or grinding. Newer burners do not have motor units. Even if you are not sure if there is one, moving the thermostat setting will give you some idea of the sound of the firing and the on and off sounds of the burner.

In an oil-fired hot air system you would have to know something about styles and types of burners to determine the approximate age of the burner "gun." If it is new or new-looking, it is very likely a high-speed, very efficient burner—but do not speculate. Ask the owner the exact age of the unit. Ask for a paid bill that describes the burner, or call and ask the oil supply company, since they probably installed it. The same would apply to an oil-fired steam or circulating hot water system.

In any oil-fueled system you should look for oil leaking around the burner and soot on the boiler or

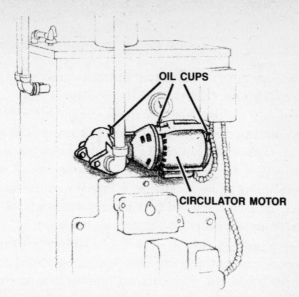

OIL CUPS

CIRCULATOR MOTOR

Hot water systems usually, but not always, have a circulating pump. It needs lubrication several times a year.

surrounding area. When the burner is turned on, sniff around for a gassy, smoky, or oily odor. A unit that misfires or spews soot will need some adjustment or repair. Any heating system that is very noisy, rumbles, or vibrates excessively will need servicing or repair. It is good practice to have any heating system turned on—winter or summer. If there is a central air-conditioning system connected to a hot air system, or if the air temperature is too high for the thermostat to react, then turning on the heat becomes a problem in the summer.

A circulating hot water system may be oil- or gas-fired. The same set of checks and observations should be made if the burner is oil-fired: sniff around for odors, noise, etc. If the unit is running, it might be a good idea to shut it off for a few minutes and then turn it back on to get some idea of its starting noise and to see if it fires immediately. A circulating hot water system usually (but not always) has a circulating pump. This would depend on the size of the building and the age and make of the boiler. If there is a pump, usually it will be located at the rear and to one side of the boiler. The pump housing is usually painted a different color from the boiler or its cover—red seems to be a favorite color. When the boiler is on, the pump should be running. It should be quiet and run smoothly—a chattering, noisy pump, or one that does not run at all, will probably need replacement. The pump should be clean-looking. There are three spots on a circulating pump that should be oiled at the beginning of the heating season. You should have the owner point them out or have a representative of the fuel supply company show them to you and explain how to take care of the boiler. If the boiler is maintained by an independent heating contractor or plumber, they should be consulted. Somewhere around the boiler of a circulating hot water system you should find an expansion tank. Look it over carefully for rusting, rust streaks, or pit marks and suspicious spots around the seams. If it has fill or drain valves, look for dripping or leaking joints or connections.

If the boiler has a tankless coil for domestic hot water (a square, iron, solid-looking box about a foot square), look for rust marks or leaking along the edges and around the seams where sections join. Sometimes you can see the edges of seals at the joints. Check around them for leaks. Of course, all plumbing and plumbing connections around the boiler should be checked for leaking.

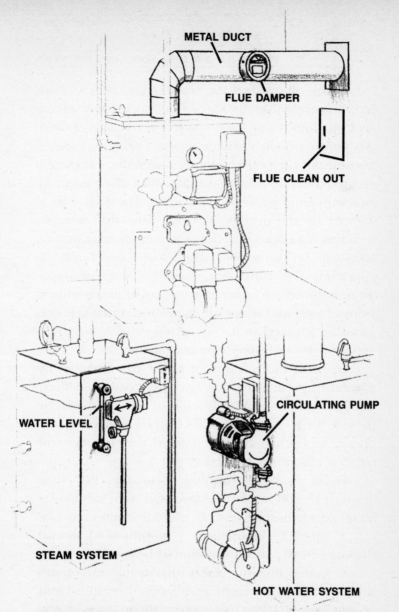

METAL DUCT

FLUE DAMPER

FLUE CLEAN OUT

WATER LEVEL

CIRCULATING PUMP

STEAM SYSTEM

HOT WATER SYSTEM

Steam systems have a water level glass, and should have a drain valve near it. Most hot water systems have no water level glass. This is one way to determine which system you have.

Check all around the heating unit where duct pipe runs from the unit to a flue or chimney. Metal ducting should not have opened seams and should not be rusted or worn through. The point where ducting goes into the chimney should be cemented around, with no openings that would allow gases to escape or blow back into the cellar. There may be a damper on the duct pipe close to the flue connection: this is a round unit with a weight on an adjusting screw along the lower edge. When the boiler is operating, the draft door should be opened about three quarters of an inch. You should make sure it swings freely and is not off its pivot and that it is not wired or jammed shut. Any problem with the draft door will mean it needs replacement.

Opening the access door to the fire chamber of a boiler (assuming that it is not sealed or bolted shut) can give you a visual indication of the condition of the fire brick or ceramic walls of the chamber. Badly broken or burned-away sections of the chamber will mean replacement is needed.

If the boiler is running or has recently shut down, it should not be touched with bare hands: the metal door(s) will be very hot and sometimes must be lifted slightly to be opened. A minimum of several thicknesses of paper towel should be used.

In older heating plants that are coal conversions, you will find small iron doors at the top front of the boiler. If you can open them without any trouble (remember, they may be very hot), you can get some indication as to how clean the boiler is and how much, if any, soot has built up internally. If the small doors resist a gentle pull, they have probably been sealed shut. Built-up soot deposits act as insulation and waste fuel, as well as affecting the efficient operation of a boiler.

The inspection of a steam system is essentially the same as for a hot water unit. The burner itself can be gas- or oil-fired and could be the same for a steam or hot water boiler. All plumbing lines and heating pipes should be checked to and from both types of boiler for leaking or dripping at joints and connections. The combustion chamber of a steam system is less likely to be sealed shut and often can be inspected through an access door. As with the hot water system, the chamber normally will be lined with fire brick and should be checked for condition. Look for broken or missing brick, excessive wear or erosion along visible surfaces, and look for any area where brick is missing or where holes and gaps allow the metal walls of the boiler sides to show. Any of these problems can mean the fire brick needs replacement. Again, be very careful because the boiler and door can be very hot. Make sure the unit is turned off and that the emergency switch is off.

As with a hot water system, the steam system may have a tankless coil for domestic hot water. If so, it should be checked for the same type of leaking at seams and seals. Of course, where the coil is inside or not accessible, visual inspection cannot be carried out.

Both the circulating hot water system and the steam boiler have visible external safety valves on top of the boiler. The hot water system usually has two together: the valve is a brass cylinder two or three inches in diameter, with a small offset arm or finger piece, and usually has a pipe inserted at an angle coming out of the side or bottom of the valve. Lifting the finger piece lightly should cause water to come out of the end of the pipe. If you don't try the valve, at least you should know where it is, so that if it ever does "blow off," you will recognize that there is a problem and you can shut the boiler off by flipping the emergency switch and calling for service.

The safety valve on a steam boiler is also set on top of the unit. It may be from three quarters of an inch to about two inches in diameter. It may be steel, chrome, or brass. The valve is cylinder-shaped and also has a small, offset lever or finger piece. Try moving the lever using very little pressure—it should move either outward and back in, or up and down. If the finger piece does not move easily or has to be pushed back to the closed position, it probably means the valve will need to be replaced.

On very old safety valves, or ones that have been tripped many times, you will find rust spots or even valves that are rusted shut. A valve that is rusted shut serves no purpose and gives a false sense of security, since it will not and cannot work when needed. If you find one rusted tight so that the finger piece will not move, the valve should be replaced immediately. The safety valve serves to blow off excess pressure; if it does not work, it could cause the boiler to explode. If you decide to try a valve for ease of operation, use a paper towel or other item between you and the metal, which could be very hot.

Again, do not exert too much pressure—if the inside of the valve or the finger piece is rusted, it could break off.

If you are testing the safety valve on a steam boiler (not a hot water unit) and water spurts out of the valve opening, then it is likely that the boiler is flooded. This may be caused by overfilling, or possibly a defective fill valve, or one that has been left turned on. You should call this to the attention of the broker or owner.

A steam boiler will have a water level glass somewhere on the exterior surface (this is one way to identify this type of heating system if you are not sure if the boiler is steam or hot water). The level glass is about eight or ten inches long and about one half inch in diameter. The condition of the water in the glass can give you some insight into the way the boiler is being maintained. Indicators of poor care are: very rusty water; a tube that looks like solid rust; or rusty water that bounces (surges) up and down. Dripping at the lower end of the level glass or encrusted mineral deposits at the connections (top or bottom) of the level glass indicate seepage and possible problems in the future.

A steam boiler should have a safety device called a "low water cutoff." This is a unit added to, or built into, the boiler that will shut down the entire boiler if the water level drops below a certain point, which is marked on the glass tube itself (always part of the casting or housing of the unit). On the unit the level marks are arrows running horizontally.

Somewhere around the level glass you should

find a round or rounded-off square, black metal unit with a valve handle jutting out at right angles over an end piece, with an opening about three quarters of an inch in diameter. This handle controls the drain valve to expel water and to clean the level glass. Turning the handle allows the water to run out of the opening below the handle. The valve handle is, or should be, spring-loaded and should close itself when released. If the valve is very rusty or if it opens with difficulty and does not shut automatically, the unit will need repair or replacement. This could mean the entire low water unit itself, not just the valve. If the low water unit is working correctly, it should make a low, but audible, click when the valve snaps shut, and the water level should return to the position on the glass that it touched before draining. If you have difficulty turning the valve, do not force it. You may not be able to shut it off, or it may break off in your hand. If you cannot find the valve, ask the owner how he takes the water out and cleans the level glass. If this is achieved by using the small drain valve under the glass tube, or at a valve low down near the floor, you are probably looking at a unit that is very old and may have been the original unit for the building. This unit may have been converted from a coal-burning boiler. You may not find a drain valve, other than under the glass tube, and you probably will not find a low water cutoff unit. The absence of this safety device will mean that the boiler should be checked every day and not left unattended if you expect to be away for more than a long weekend. Installation of a safety unit on a very old or converted boiler may not be possible.

In the long run you may find the cost of repairs, maintenance, and upgrading to a fifty-year-old boiler, plus its inefficient operation, too expensive when compared to the heat it supplies versus the fuel and effort put in. You should probably estimate having to add the cost of a new boiler to the price of the building.

Steam systems lose a certain amount of water, either through the radiator air valve as dissipated steam, or where steam in radiators and risers condenses back to water and is partly dried out or evaporated in return lines or other hot pipes. Because of this, water will have to be added to the boiler occasionally to raise the water level. This shows up in the gauge glass. Water is usually added manually, by partly opening a fill valve located somewhere in the boiler's plumbing system. The valve is found close to the boiler and, in many instances, will have a marked tag. Boilers can also be filled with a controlled device located within the same boiler plumbing system: this is an "automatic water feed"; some of them have a label that identifies the control as such.

An automatic water feed unit may come in a variety of shapes or sizes, from one that is small, rectangular, and made of aluminum and iron; or a steel box; to a melon-size, mostly round black ball. Some units have a button on top, which enables you to override the unit and add water to the boiler over and above the "normal" level marked. If you have been told there is an automatic water feed and cannot find it, ask the owner to identify it for you.

You can check an automatic water feed unit to see if it is working by draining water out of the boiler at the drain valve near the level glass or by finding the boiler drain valve near the bottom of the boiler and removing water through it. If you use the lower valve, you may have to drain quite a lot of water before the automatic water feed responds and starts to refill the boiler. Usually you only have to take enough water out of the unit to drop the water level in the glass tube below the center point. If the automatic feed is working correctly, the water level should be returned to the mark where it was before draining.

If there is no drain valve around the level glass (as in some coal conversions), then water has to be removed from the boiler or the level glass by using the lower drain valve or a valve on one of the pipes at the bottom of the unit. Water can be removed from a level glass to clean out rust by using the small brass valve at the bottom of the glass tube. This can be dangerous, since the water is very hot and there is a possibility of breaking the glass. Unless you have a new glass and know how to replace it, you should leave it to the service person to drain and clean.

The inside of the glass tube can become very rough because of rust and water bouncing around, and many times the water level cannot be seen clearly because of the "etched" effect.

To add to the confusion, sometimes there is a vacuum pump connected within the system. Unless you have a fairly large range of experience, the only thing that you should be checking for are obvious items, such as leaking in or around the boiler, rusty connections or controls, and anything appearing suspicious or out of the ordinary. If the unit is operating at the time of your inspection, listen for odd noises and sniff around for odd smells.

V.
Checklist

After having read through this entire book you should be better prepared to look at a building with a more objective approach.

The checklist should be helpful even though you may be taking other notes as you go along. You should always start out with a pad, a pen, and a flashlight, plus a magnet and a screwdriver. You might carry a small tape recorder, though it sometimes looks like you are talking to yourself rather than the machine. If you are looking at a suburban property where you cannot get onto a roof, or if you are looking at a building with a pitched roof, a pair of binoculars will help.

In recent years there have been new problems that have surfaced in the ownership and/or purchase of a home. At the height of the fuel crisis, insulating the walls of a building became important as everyone became conservation aware. One of the big problems that resulted from this was the use of urea foam insulation. A short time after its popularity and use, it was deemed to be a cancer-causing agent, went off the market, and then returned with a different formulation. The government banned the use of urea foam insulation with its original formula and then allowed its use again after the formula was changed. Many houses that used the original foam could not be sold until the foam insulation was removed. This meant the demolition of inside walls and replacement after the foam was taken out.

Most of the heating pipes in cellars have had or still have some degree of asbestos insulation; many old furnaces are still partly coated with asbestos cement; a lot of the asbestos insulation is flaking off and loose in many cellars; and recent findings show that asbestos is a cancer-causing agent. The same material is found in resilient floor tiles and other materials in and around buildings.

There are sections of the country that are in radon belts. Radon is the breakdown of natural radioactive material in the ground, and this also has been shown to be a cancer-causing agent.

If you have any concerns about any of the possible toxic effects of any of the above materials, you will have to question the owner, the broker, and possibly the local town or municipal engineer's office for any available information. Other than asbestos, there is no obvious indication of the other materials: foam is hidden in walls and radon is an invisible gas.

CHECKLIST

EXTERIOR

SIDEWALK   Yes_____   No_____
                 Condition_____

DRIVEWAY   Yes_____   No_____
                 Condition_____

OVERHEAD
ELECTRIC
LINES   Yes_____   No_____

ROOF   Good_____   Fair_____   Poor_____
  Leaders
  Gutters   Good_____   Fair_____   Poor_____
                 Copper_____   Aluminum_____
                 Galvanized_____
  Type   Slate_____   Ceramic tile_____
                 Wood shingles_____
                 Asphalt shingles_____
                 Roll roofing_____
                 Tar and gravel_____
                 Metal roofing_____
  Flashing   Aluminum_____   Copper_____
                 Tarred over_____
                 Condition_____

Roof problems
  Chimney(s)

                     Good _____   Fair _____   Poor _____
                     Brick _____   Masonry _____
                     Metal _____   Lined _____

WALLS   Good _____   Fair _____   Poor _____
                     Paint _____   Stained _____
                     Natural finish _____

TRIM   Good _____   Fair _____   Poor _____
                     Paint _____

  Vents
    (Gables) Yes _____   No _____
  Vents
    (Soffits) Yes _____   No _____

Additional comments and observations _____

_____

_____

_____

DOORS   Good _____   Fair _____   Poor _____
  Fit   Good _____   Fair _____   Poor _____
  Caulking Good _____   Fair _____   Poor _____
  Storm
    door(s) Yes _____   No _____   Number _____
                     Good _____   Fair _____   Poor _____

STORM WINDOWS AND SCREENS

Yes_____   No_____
Good_____   Fair_____   Poor_____

**Windows
other than
storms**   Good_____   Fair_____   Poor_____

Additional comments and observations_____

_____

_____
_____

GARAGE   Yes_____   No_____   No. of cars_____
Attached_____   Detached_____
Heat_____   Light_____   Outlet_____
Water_____
Door   Roll-up_____   Hinged_____
Electric opener_____
Good_____   Fair_____   Poor_____

STAIRS   Brick_____   Stone_____
Mixed_____   Wood_____
Other_____
Good_____   Fair_____   Poor_____

PORCH
Condition: Front_____   Side_____
Rear_____   Side_____

**FIRE
ESCAPE**   Yes_____   No_____

               Good_____   Fair_____   Poor_____

  Paint

    Condition: Good_____   Fair_____   Poor_____

OUTBUILDING(S)_____

Additional comments and observations_____

_____

_____

_____

INTERIOR
CELLARS
  Support
    walls   Cracks_____   Shift_____
                     Bulging_____   Stained_____
                     Wet_____   Damp_____
  Floor   Good_____   Fair_____   Poor_____
                     Cracks_____   Shift_____
                     Bulge_____
                     Above_____   Below grade_____
  Finished
    walls   Yes_____   No_____
                     Good_____   Fair_____   Poor_____
  Ceiling
    Finished: Yes_____   No_____
                     Good_____   Fair_____   Poor_____
  Joists   Spacing_____
                     Good_____   Fair_____   Poor_____
  Posts or
    columns   Good_____   Fair_____   Poor_____
  Crawl areas   Vents: Yes_____   No_____
                     Insulation: Yes_____   No_____
  Termite (or other insect) or rot damage
                     Yes_____   No_____
  Location of damage_____

Additional comments and observations_____
_____
_____
_____

Sump pump Yes_____ No_____

Water damage to floor(s)

     Yes_____ No_____

     Stained_____ Wet_____

 Floor drain(s)

     Yes_____ No_____

GAS SERVICE IN BUILDING

     Yes_____ No_____

Supplied by utility co.

     Yes_____ No_____

Bottled gas Yes_____ No_____

SEWER
SYSTEM Septic system_____ Cesspool_____

     Municipal system_____

WATER Municipal system_____ Well_____

Water

 softener Yes_____ No_____

     Age_____

Well   Yes_____ No_____

     Dug_____ Drilled_____

     Good_____ Fair_____ Poor_____

Pressure at faucets

     Good_____ Fair_____ Poor_____

Water appearance_____
Taste_____
Storage tank

        Yes_____   No_____

        Good_____   Fair_____   Poor_____

Pump or other components of well system service

        Yes_____   No_____

Cesspool or septic system service

        Yes_____   No_____

Additional comments and observations_____

_____

_____

_____

HEATING
SYSTEM
Hot water

Steam_____   Forced air_____
Electric_____   Gas-fueled_____
Oil_____   Electric_____   Solar_____
Wood_____   Coal_____

Condition of heating plant

Good_____   Fair_____   Poor_____
Leaking_____   Sooty_____
Rusty_____   Smell_____   Drips_____

CENTRAL AIR-CONDITIONING

Appearance   Good_____   Fair_____   Poor_____

Working_____   Noisy_____
Rusty_____   Age_____

Service contract on heating system

Yes_____   No_____
Runs out_____

Service contract on air conditioner unit

Yes_____   No_____
Runs out_____

Additional comments and observations on heating and cooling units_____

_____

_____

_____

HOT WATER PROVIDED BY_____

Tankless coil connected to boiler

                        Yes_____   No_____

Leaking   Yes_____   No_____

Separate detached hot water tank

                        Yes_____   No_____

Fueled by   Gas_____   Oil_____

                        Electricity_____

Capacity   _____Gals.

Rusty seams Yes_____   No_____

Dripping   Yes_____   No_____

Leaking   Yes_____   No_____

Burn or scorch marks at bottom area of tank

                        Yes_____   No_____

PLUMBING SYSTEM

Water supply pipe coming into the building

                    Lead_____   Copper_____

                    Brass_____   Iron_____   Plastic_____

Leaking   Yes_____   No_____

Dripping   Yes_____   No_____

Shutoff valve leaking or dripping

                        Yes_____   No_____

Water meter Yes_____   No_____

Piping throughout the cellar/basement

    Copper_____   Brass_____

    Iron_____   Plastic_____

    Lead_____

    Mixed_____

    Location(s) of mixed pipe_____

Rust marks   Yes_____   No_____
            Location_____
Dripping or leaking joints or connections
            Yes_____   No_____
            Location_____

Shutoff valves
            Yes_____   No_____
            Good_____   Fair_____   Poor_____
Sprinkler main (multiple dwelling)
            Iron_____   Brass_____
            Copper_____
Condition at entry into building
            Good_____   Fair_____   Poor_____
Condition of shutoff valve
     Dripping or leaking
            Yes_____   No_____
Visible dripping to joints or connections
            Yes_____   No_____
            Location_____

Dripping or condensation along plumbing lines
            Yes_____   No_____

WASTE SYSTEM
Plumbing   Cast iron_____
                Galvanized steel or iron_____
                Copper_____   Plastic_____
Rusting   Yes_____   No_____
Leaking at joints
                Yes_____   No_____
Clean-out trap (pit) condition
                Good_____   Fair_____   Poor_____
  Wet or backing up
                Yes_____   No_____

**Additional comments and observations on water and
waste systems**_____
_____
_____
_____

ELECTRICAL SYSTEM
Main fuse or circuit breaker marked for
                _____Amps   _____Volts
Fuses   Yes_____   No_____
Circuit breakers
                Yes_____   No_____
Number of fuses_____
Number of circuit breakers_____
B.X. cable   Yes_____   No_____
Conduit   Yes_____   No_____
Plastic   Yes_____   No_____
  If plastic, is it marked copper_____ or
  aluminum_____

Condition of visible cable, conduit, or plastic
(Romex) Good_____ Fair_____ Poor_____
Condition of cellar or basement light fixtures
                Good_____ Fair_____ Poor_____

Additional comments and observations on the electrical system_____
_____
_____
_____

ROOM (Identify)_____

Ceiling condition

    Good_____ Fair_____ Poor_____

 Material_____

Walls condition

    Good_____ Fair_____ Poor_____

 Material_____

Floor type Wood_____ Resilient tile_____

      Linoleum_____ Carpet_____

      Other_____

Condition_____

Electrical outlets (number)_____

Air conditioner outlet

    Yes_____ No_____

Wall switch_____ **Pull chain**_____

Grounded outlets

    All_____ Some_____

Closet(s) Lights: Yes_____ No_____

Heat   Yes_____ No_____

 Permanent_____ Added portable_____

Window condition prime unit

    Good_____ Fair_____ Poor_____

Storm window

    Yes_____ No_____

    Good_____ Fair_____ Poor_____

Fit of doors, trim, windows_____

Additional comments and observations_____

_____

_____

_____

BATHROOM   Full_____   Half_____
  Plumbing
    type   Copper_____   Brass_____
                 Iron_____   Plastic_____
                 Lead_____
  Water
    pressure Good_____   Fair_____   Poor_____
  Floor   Tile_____   Wood_____
                 Linoleum_____   Resilient tile_____
                 Good_____   Fair_____   Poor_____
  Wall tile Yes_____   No_____
                 Good_____   Fair_____   Poor_____
  Upper bathroom walls
                 Good_____   Fair_____   Poor_____
  Bathroom ceiling
                 Good_____   Fair_____   Poor_____
  Bathroom
    light   Yes_____   No_____
  Electrical
    outlet   Yes_____   No_____

Additional comments and observations on bathroom

_____

_____

_____

ROOM (Identify)_____

Ceiling condition
                    Good_____   Fair_____   Poor_____
    Material_____
Walls condition
                    Good_____   Fair_____   Poor_____
    Material_____
Floor type   Wood_____   Resilient tile_____
                  Linoleum_____   Carpet_____
                  Other_____
Condition_____
Electrical outlets (number)_____
Air conditioner outlet
                    Yes_____   No_____
Wall switch_____   **Pull chain**_____
Grounded outlets
                    All_____   Some_____
Closet(s)   Lights: Yes_____   No_____
Heat   Yes_____   No_____
    Permanent_____   Added portable_____
Window condition prime unit
                    Good_____   Fair_____   Poor_____
Storm window
                    Yes_____   No_____
                    Good_____   Fair_____   Poor_____
Fit of doors, trim, windows_____

Additional comments and observations_____
_____
_____
_____

BATHROOM   Full＿＿   Half＿＿

  Plumbing

    type   Copper＿＿   Brass＿＿

              Iron＿＿   Plastic＿＿

              Lead＿＿

  Water

    pressure Good＿＿   Fair＿＿   Poor＿＿

  Floor   Tile＿＿   Wood＿＿

              Linoleum＿＿   Resilient tile＿＿

              Good＿＿   Fair＿＿   Poor＿＿

  Wall tile Yes＿＿   No＿＿

              Good＿＿   Fair＿＿   Poor＿＿

  Upper bathroom walls

              Good＿＿   Fair＿＿   Poor＿＿

  Bathroom ceiling

              Good＿＿   Fair＿＿   Poor＿＿

  Bathroom

    light   Yes＿＿   No＿＿

  Electrical

    outlet   Yes＿＿   No＿＿

Additional comments and observations on bathroom

_____

_____

_____

ROOM (Identify)_____

   Ceiling condition

                  Good_____ Fair_____ Poor_____

   Material_____

   Walls condition

                  Good_____ Fair_____ Poor_____

   Material_____

   Floor type   Wood_____   Resilient tile_____

                  Linoleum_____ Carpet_____

                  Other_____

   Condition_____

   Electrical outlets (number)_____

   Air conditioner outlet

                  Yes_____ No_____

   Wall switch_____   **Pull chain**_____

   Grounded outlets

                  All_____ Some_____

   Closet(s) Lights: Yes_____ No_____

   Heat   Yes_____ No_____

   Permanent_____ Added portable_____

   Window condition prime unit

                  Good_____ Fair_____ Poor_____

   Storm window

                  Yes_____ No_____

                  Good_____ Fair_____ Poor_____

   Fit of doors, trim, windows_____

Additional comments and observations_____

_____

_____

_____

BATHROOM　　Full＿＿＿　　Half＿＿＿

Plumbing

   type　　　Copper＿＿＿　　Brass＿＿＿

            Iron＿＿＿　　Plastic＿＿＿

            Lead＿＿＿

Water

   pressure　　Good＿＿＿　　Fair＿＿＿　　Poor＿＿＿

Floor　　　　Tile＿＿＿　　Wood＿＿＿

            Linoleum＿＿＿　　Resilient tile＿＿＿

            Good＿＿＿　　Fair＿＿＿　　Poor＿＿＿

Wall tile　　Yes＿＿＿　　No＿＿＿

            Good＿＿＿　　Fair＿＿＿　　Poor＿＿＿

Upper bathroom walls

            Good＿＿＿　　Fair＿＿＿　　Poor＿＿＿

Bathroom ceiling

            Good＿＿＿　　Fair＿＿＿　　Poor＿＿＿

Bathroom

   light　　　Yes＿＿＿　　No＿＿＿

Electrical

   outlet　　Yes＿＿＿　　No＿＿＿

Additional comments and observations on bathroom

＿＿＿＿＿＿＿＿＿＿＿＿＿＿＿＿＿＿＿＿＿＿＿＿＿＿

＿＿＿＿＿＿＿＿＿＿＿＿＿＿＿＿＿＿＿＿＿＿＿＿＿＿

＿＿＿＿＿＿＿＿＿＿＿＿＿＿＿＿＿＿＿＿＿＿＿＿＿＿

ROOM (Identify)_____

    Ceiling condition

                 Good_____ Fair_____ Poor_____

    Material_____

    Walls condition

                 Good_____ Fair_____ Poor_____

    Material_____

    Floor type   Wood_____ Resilient tile_____

                   Linoleum_____ Carpet_____

                   Other_____

    Condition_____

    Electrical outlets (number)_____

    Air conditioner outlet

                 Yes_____ No_____

    Wall switch_____ **Pull chain**_____

    Grounded outlets

                 All_____ Some_____

    Closet(s) Lights: Yes_____ No_____

    Heat   Yes_____ No_____

    Permanent_____ Added portable_____

    Window condition prime unit

                 Good_____ Fair_____ Poor_____

    Storm window

                 Yes_____ No_____

                 Good_____ Fair_____ Poor_____

    Fit of doors, trim, windows_____

Additional comments and observations_____

_____

_____

_____

BATHROOM   Full ____   Half ____

Plumbing
   type   Copper ____   Brass ____
             Iron ____   Plastic ____
             Lead ____

Water
   pressure   Good ____   Fair ____   Poor ____

Floor   Tile ____   Wood ____
             Linoleum ____   Resilient tile ____
             Good ____   Fair ____   Poor ____

Wall tile   Yes ____   No ____
             Good ____   Fair ____   Poor ____

Upper bathroom walls
             Good ____   Fair ____   Poor ____

Bathroom ceiling
             Good ____   Fair ____   Poor ____

Bathroom
   light   Yes ____   No ____

Electrical
   outlet   Yes ____   No ____

Additional comments and observations on bathroom

_____

_____

_____

ROOM (Identify)_____

Ceiling condition

Good_____ Fair_____ Poor_____

Material_____

Walls condition

Good_____ Fair_____ Poor_____

Material_____

Floor type Wood_____ Resilient tile_____

Linoleum_____ Carpet_____

Other_____

Condition_____

Electrical outlets (number)_____

Air conditioner outlet

Yes_____ No_____

Wall switch_____ **Pull chain**_____

Grounded outlets

All_____ Some_____

Closet(s) Lights: Yes_____ No_____

Heat   Yes_____ No_____

Permanent_____ Added portable_____

Window condition prime unit

Good_____ Fair_____ Poor_____

Storm window

Yes_____ No_____

Good_____ Fair_____ Poor_____

Fit of doors, trim, windows_____

Additional comments and observations_____

_____

_____

_____

BATHROOM   Full_____   Half_____
Plumbing
   type   Copper_____   Brass_____
           Iron_____   Plastic_____
           Lead_____

Water
   pressure   Good_____   Fair_____   Poor_____
Floor   Tile_____   Wood_____
           Linoleum_____   Resilient tile_____
           Good_____   Fair_____   Poor_____
Wall tile   Yes_____   No_____
           Good_____   Fair_____   Poor_____

Upper bathroom walls
           Good_____   Fair_____   Poor_____

Bathroom ceiling
           Good_____   Fair_____   Poor_____

Bathroom
   light   Yes_____   No_____
Electrical
   outlet   Yes_____   No_____

Additional comments and observations on bathroom

_____

_____

_____

ATTIC   Yes_____   No_____
  Crawl space   Yes_____   No_____
  Ladder_____   **Stairs**_____
  Pull down staircase_____
    Condition: Good_____   Fair_____   Poor_____
  Stains or leak marks: Roof boards_____
    Framing_____   Other wood areas_____
  Leaks or stains around chimney or
  vent pipes_____
  Attic
    window   Yes_____   No_____
          Good_____   Fair_____   Poor_____
  Insulation   Floor_____   Walls_____
          Type_____
  Electrical cable or wire condition
          Good_____   Fair_____   Poor_____
  Lighting   Yes_____   No_____
  Outlet   Yes_____   No_____
  Attic fan   Yes_____   No_____
    Working   Yes_____   No_____
  Full floor   Yes_____   No_____
  Walk-around attic
          Yes_____   No_____
  Low ceiling storage only_____

Additional comments and observations_____
_____
_____
_____

HALLS

Walls	Good_____	Fair_____	Poor_____
Ceilings	Good_____	Fair_____	Poor_____
1st flr	Good_____	Fair_____	Poor_____
2nd flr	Good_____	Fair_____	Poor_____
3rd flr	Good_____	Fair_____	Poor_____
4th flr	Good_____	Fair_____	Poor_____

STAIRS

1st flr	Good_____	Fair_____	Poor_____
2nd flr	Good_____	Fair_____	Poor_____
3rd flr	Good_____	Fair_____	Poor_____
4th flr	Good_____	Fair_____	Poor_____
Handrails	Yes_____	No_____	
Good_____	Fair_____	Poor_____	
Posts	_____		
Good_____	Fair_____	Poor_____	
Spindles			
Good_____	Fair_____	Poor_____	

Additional comments and observations on stairs

_____

_____

_____

INDEX